The Art of Ministry

(A Handbook of Practical Ministry)

Dag Heward-Mills

Parchment House

THE ART OF MINISTRY

Copyright © 2014 Dag Heward-Mills

First published 2014 by Parchment House
16th printing 2016

Find out more about Dag Heward-Mills at:

Healing Jesus Campaign
Write to: evangelist@daghewardmills.org
Website: www.daghewardmills.org
Facebook: Dag Heward-Mills
Twitter: @EvangelistDag

ISBN 13: 978-1-61395-483-6

Dedication

To

Johnny Awanyo and Oko Bortei-Doku

Johnny, thank you for years of fixing my "plugs", building the best ever choirs
and making music work in the church. Since you said "yes" in school, you
have done every kind of church work and

Oko, thank you for being the life and joy of our office and embracing full-time
ministry as the greatest opportunity to serve God. Thank you for being a
personal assistant to me and for pastoring and fathering our children.

Contents

Chapter 1

The Gifts and Calling of God are without Repentance

The First Call

Now the word of the LORD came unto Jonah the son of Amittai, saying, Arise, go to Nineveh, that great city, and cry against it; for their wickedness is come up before me.

Jonah 1:1-2

The Second Call

And the word of the LORD came unto Jonah THE SECOND TIME, saying, Arise, go unto Nineveh, that great city, and preach unto it the preaching that I bid thee.

Jonah 3:1-2

God is a God of mercy! He will give you a second chance to obey Him. Jonah is an example of someone who had a second chance to hear and obey. Sometimes we have only one chance!

The God of a Second Chance

Perhaps, God has always wanted you to work in a church and that is why He created you. Perhaps you have been running away from God's call. But God is speaking to you again. God spoke to Jonah twice. In between the first and second calls, Jonah had many experiences. He experienced the storms of life and the prison of the whale's belly. Perhaps after many hard experiences, you are ready to listen to God.

Perhaps as you hold this book, God is giving you a second chance to work in His house. It is time to join the army for the last battle.

No Change in the Call

You will notice that the first call and the second call were identical. In both the first and the second calls, Jonah was sent to the same city (Nineveh) with exactly the same message. The gifts and calling of God are without repentance (Romans 11:29).

God does not change His mind with the passage of time. Even after you have experienced the pain of storms and whales; bellies, He can still use you. Ten years may have passed since God first began to call you. It is not too late to obey Him. I am glad I serve the God who never changes His mind.

Accepting the call of God is accepting to be made into something that you are not. Jesus offered to make Peter into what he was not - a fisher of men!

Coming into the ministry is not about making some great contribution to the kingdom of God. Nothing depends on you and nothing will be destroyed by you neglecting the ministry. We are all expendable and dispensable.

For we can do nothing against the truth, but for the truth.

2 Corinthians 13:8

This Scripture teaches us that there is nothing we can ever do that will go against the truth of God's Word. Our greatest mistakes will not hinder the truth of the Gospel. Greatly neglecting our call cannot change the course of God's triumphant army. It is our privilege to be called to this work. It is our honour to be involved. It is time to stop thinking that you are going to do something unusual for God.

Being in the ministry is a humbling experience in which you actually learn about God and receive mercy. Jesus told His disciples to follow Him and He would make them into something. In full-time ministry, you will be moulded into a vessel God can use.

And Jesus said unto them, Come ye after me, and I WILL MAKE you to become fishers of men.

Mark 1:17

In full-time ministry, you will be transformed by the renewing of your mind and by the numerous humbling experiences that await you. Full-time ministry is actually the beginning of a journey that brings you closer to God. It changes you and makes you a humble person. The very nature of this despised work and the interaction with other Christians in ministry will surely break you down and make you a better person! Also, the interaction with outsiders who do not understand what full-time ministry is about will drive you deeper into God.

What Full-Time Ministry Is Not

Being in full-time ministry is when Jesus makes you into "fishers of men". Being paid by the ministry does not necessarily make you a full-time minister.

Switching your source of salary from the bank to the church does not mean you are in full-time ministry. Full-time ministry is an all-encompassing step in which you follow the Lord absolutely. Your following Him will mean many things, including some of the points listed below.

Full-time ministry is not as simple as switching jobs. It is a lifetime commitment. It will swallow your whole being and you will be transformed by the power of God.

Full-time ministry is not any of these:

- Full-time ministry is not a convenient job option.

- Full-time ministry is not an easier job option.

- Full-time ministry is not a retirement plan for the elderly.

- Full-time ministry is not an arrangement for redeployed workers.

- Full-time ministry is not a refuge for mothers of little children.

- Full-time ministry is not a last-minute death wish for people who have spent their better years doing other things.

- Full-time ministry is not a camouflaged business plan. Some people want to use full-time ministry to ensure a regular salary whilst they do their businesses on the side. Business is business and ministry is ministry!

- Full-time ministry is not an activity for people in between jobs.

- Full-time ministry is not a springboard for men with secular ambitions.

- Full-time ministry is not a poverty alleviation scheme. Sometimes it is financially better to work in the ministry.

- Full-time ministry is not the same as transferring your profession from the secular world to the church. The fact that you were an accountant in the world does not mean that you must be an accountant in the church.

- Full-time ministry is not just about switching your source of salary.

- Full-time ministry is not a vacation job. Full-time ministry is not something for students to do to whilst on holiday.

Delusions about Full-Time Ministry

There are common current state delusions that plague people in different circumstances. People in full-time ministry are not spared their share of delusions. Some of the delusions that afflict a full-time minister are:

1. Because I am in full-time ministry I am special.

2. Because I am in full-time ministry I will have a good salary.

3. Because I am in full-time ministry I have taken the highest spiritual step and there are no more spiritual steps to be taken.

4. Because I am in full-time ministry I am better than lay ministers.

5. Because I am in full-time ministry I will travel to foreign countries.

6. Because I am in full-time ministry I will have a big house.

7. Because I am in full-time ministry I will have a car.

8. Because I am in full-time ministry I will be rich.

9. Because I am in full-time ministry I have become spiritual.

10. Because I am in full-time ministry I will have a better marriage and a better family life.

11. Because I am in full-time ministry I will have more time to pray, worship and study the Word.

12. Because I am in full-time ministry God is very pleased with me.

13. Because I am in full-time ministry I am walking in love.

14. Because I am in full-time ministry my judgment will be easy.

15. Because I am in full-time ministry I am anointed and protected.

16. Because I am in full-time ministry my children will turn out very well.

17. Because I am in full-time ministry I will go to Heaven by all means.

18. Because I am in full-time ministry I am loyal.

None of the things listed above are necessarily true. They may be true, but many of them may not be true in your case. And they are definitely not things that will happen automatically. You must seek God in full-time ministry so that all His plans will come to pass.

Chapter 2

The Difference between Secular Work and Ministry Work

There Is a Difference

**But they will become his slaves so that they may
LEARN THE DIFFERENCE between My service and
the service of the kingdoms of the countries.**

2 Chronicles 12:8, NASB

When Rehoboam rebelled against God, the prophet sent him a chilling message. He told him he would show him the difference between working for God and working for the nations of the world.

There is a difference between working for God and working for the world. Amassing wealth in this fading world cannot be compared with the high calling of God.

To build an eternal city with real foundations is the highest privilege for mortal man. Most men spend their lives building temporary things which have no future. The average man is simply a builder of temporal sandcastles.

Who Is Pharaoh?

Pharaoh is a "type" of Satan. Egypt is a "type" of the world and Israel is a "type" of God's people. Pharaoh afflicted God's people with hard labour and made them build treasure cities. This clearly depicts secular work today.

Most of the time spent in the secular world is spent building the cities of this world. By the time we are dead and gone, we have only added more beautiful buildings to the skyline of this world's cities.

The work of this world is with much rigour, much tension and much sweat. We are made to work harder and harder without realizing that we are actually building the treasure cities of this world. New York City, Paris, London, Accra, Lagos and Nairobi were built with the sweat of hard-working human beings.

These human beings are dead and gone but the treasure cities remain. Their life's work may be summed up as a contribution to the development of the treasure cities of the world. Mind you, Satan said to Jesus when he showed Him the nations of this world:

All this power will I give thee, and the glory of them: for that is delivered unto me; and to whomsoever I will I give it.

Luke 4:6

This shows us that it is actually Satan who exercises power over the cities of this world. The devil is the god of this world (2 Corinthians 4:4). It is Satan who has given the sons of men much hard labour and guided them to build the cities of this world.

Christians simply join the army of builders and contribute their quota to build these treasure cities.

Now there arose up a new king over Egypt, which knew not Joseph.
And he said unto his people, Behold, the people of the children of Israel are more and mightier than we:
Come on, let us deal wisely with them; lest they multiply, and it come to pass, that, when there falleth out any war, they join also unto our enemies, and fight against us, and so get them up out of the land.
Therefore they did set over them taskmasters to afflict them with their burdens. And they built for Pharaoh treasure cities, Pithom and Raamses.
But the more they afflicted them, the more they multiplied and grew. And they were grieved because of the children of Israel.

And the Egyptians made the children of Israel to serve with rigour:

Exodus 1:8-13

Just as Pharaoh controlled Egypt, Satan controls the world and its cities. That is why the entropy and confusion of this world is increasing steadily to its climax.

When you work in the financial institutions, banks and other secular organizations of this world, you can be compared to the Israelites working for Pharaoh; there is much rigour, much tension and much sweat about building sandcastles.

Moses requested that the people of Israel be set free so that they could serve the Lord. Anyone desiring to come into full-time ministry finds himself requesting a departure from the world system. Full-time ministry is service to the Lord! It is like going away from Egypt and into the desert to sacrifice to the Lord and build Him a tabernacle!

God wants His people to spend their time building Him a tabernacle and worshipping Him.

Of course, escaping from the world system is not going to be easy. It was not easy for Moses and the children of Israel to leave Egypt. It was only through a determined struggle that the people of God finally escaped from Pharaoh.

Dear friend, it will not be easy for you to escape from secular work. If it happens it will be through much struggle.

Four Stages for Escape from Pharaoh

And it came to pass, when PHARAOH WOULD HARDLY LET US GO...

Exodus 13:15

Pharaoh was not pleased to let the children of Israel go free. There are four stages that every Christian may go through in order to break out into full-time ministry. You must recognize each of these situations when you are presented with them.

Stage 1: *Pharaoh does not want you to leave his employment.*

And Pharaoh said, Who is the Lord, that I should obey his voice to let Israel go? I know not the Lord, NEITHER WILL I LET ISRAEL GO.

Exodus 5:2

Pharaoh wants you to work for him until you are dead. He wants you to sweat and toil until you die. Satan knows that many people will never reach the retirement age. He deludes them into working towards an imaginary retirement which will never materialize.

Stage 2: *Pharaoh will allow you to serve God but wants you to remain with him.*

And Pharaoh called for Moses and for Aaron, and said, Go ye, sacrifice to your God IN THE LAND.

Exodus 8:25

In this next stage, Pharaoh yields to some pressure. He agrees that you should serve God but you must remain in Egypt. You must continue to build Pharaoh's pyramids. This form of service is politely called the lay ministry. Serving God, but well fastened to the world system of earning money!

Pharaoh will prescribe when you can go to church and when you cannot. Once you are in his land, you belong to him and he decides everything you do. He decides when you wake up and when you go to bed. He decides what you do everyday of the week. He leaves you with only Sundays to relax but sometimes he will take even that from you.

Why should Pharaoh tell you to serve God only on Sunday afternoons and Wednesday evenings? Why can't you serve God on Monday mornings as well? Why should Pharaoh control what I do on Tuesdays, Wednesdays, Thursdays and Fridays? When Moses led the people of Israel to the wilderness, they were free to serve the Lord exclusively.

This is the ultimate desire of God for every one of His children. Sadly though, very few ever get to this state of perfect liberation from Pharaoh and all that he represents.

Stage 3: *Pharaoh does not want you to go too far.*

And Pharaoh said, I will let you go, that ye may sacrifice to the LORD your God in the wilderness; ONLY YE SHALL NOT GO VERY FAR away: intreat for me.

Exodus 8:28

In stage three, you are warned not to go too far with God and the ministry. Many Christians side with Pharaoh at this stage.

Good and moral Christians will warn of the dangers of extremism. Today's church is full of "Mr Good" and "Mrs. Perfect" who are neither hot nor cold. It is a church of "mature," moral, never-do-wrong Christians who neither go too far nor too near! "Mr. Clean" is neither hot nor cold!

Something in between will do! When you suggest the idea of full-time ministry, they say you should not go too far.

Stage 4: *Pharaoh does not want you to risk your finances in ministry.*

And Pharaoh called unto Moses, and said, Go ye, serve the Lord; ONLY LET YOUR FLOCKS AND YOUR HERDS BE STAYED: let your little ones also go with you.

Exodus 10:24

Today's lukewarm Christians want to serve God without risking anything. They fully agree with Pharaoh's suggestion about serving the Lord without risking their businesses or their earthly possessions.

The modern church, including the modern pastor, is amazed at the idea of professionals leaving their vocations for the ministry. What a glorious honour it is to receive an invitation of the Lord to build His tabernacle!

Yet, the voices of the ones who are neither hot nor cold drown the voice of the Spirit. They say, "Don't risk your life, don't risk the flocks, and don't risk your resources on a crazy adventure. Don't follow this crazy man."

Dear friend, there is no higher calling than to serve the King of Kings. Fight your way out of prison. Make it your life's ambition to follow the pillar of cloud and the pillar of fire. Make it your life's work to build His tabernacle rather than building the treasure cities of Pharaoh.

Chapter 3

What it Means to Walk Worthy of Your Calling

...walk in a manner worthy of the calling with which you have been called,

Ephesians 4:1, NASB

The Apostle warns us all to walk in a manner worthy of the calling. I became a medical doctor in 1989. I had been in medical school for seven long years. It was a strange feeling to suddenly be a "respected" medical doctor. I had been a student for so long.

For the last twenty-five years of my life, I had been treated as a "young" student. Now, I was a "prestigious" doctor. I couldn't do some of the things I did before. I had to live up to the new and esteemed image of a medical doctor.

So it is with ministry. God wants you to live up to your new vocation of full-time ministry. You must endeavour to accomplish all that God has desired for you.

Understand Why You Must Walk Worthy

1. You must walk worthy because it is a privilege to be chosen.

Therefore seeing we have this ministry, as WE HAVE RECEIVED MERCY, we faint not.

2 Corinthians 4:1

It is truly a privilege to be chosen by the Lord. To be saved is the highest privilege a human being could have. When I consider the millions of people who live and die, never knowing the Lord, I consider it my greatest blessing to be saved.

When I consider my friends and relatives who do not know the Lord, I am eternally grateful for my salvation. What more could I ask for? Yet there seems to be something higher that God is giving to some of us - a call to full-time ministry! This truly is the mercy of God. That is why you must walk worthy. To work for God is the opportunity very few people in this world will ever have.

2. You must walk worthy because you have a limited season of opportunity.

This is what applies to the Levites: from twenty-five years old and upward they shall enter to perform service in the work of the tent of meeting.

But at the age of fifty years they shall retire from service in the work and not work any more.

Numbers 8:24-25, NASB

From the Scripture above, a short period is allotted for the work of ministry. Some people delay unduly and lose their opportunity to work for God. It is a blessing if you responded to this call in time. It takes the grace of God to respond in time or even to respond at all!

If you find yourself working in a church, be thankful and behave yourself wisely because it is a privilege.

3. You must walk worthy because the grace of God has worked for you.

By the grace of God I am what I am...

1 Corinthians 15:10

It takes the grace of God to even hear the call. It takes the grace of God to respond appropriately to the call of God. Most human beings do not respond appropriately to the call. Jonah messed things up and had to be swallowed by a whale. Moses could not accept his call until Aaron was brought into the picture.

Many people stay away from ministry because they do not know what their calling is. Some simply do not have the opportunity to work in a church. Paul said, "I am what I am by the grace of God." How true that is!

Coming into full-time ministry can be very complicated. Parents and friends are likely to oppose the ministry. I struggled to enter full-time ministry. I tried business and other ventures. I tried to go to America to be close to a man of God so I could learn from him. None of these things worked out. When my father found out that I was not planning on becoming a specialist doctor, he warned me and told me I was on my own. Through the financial help of my sister I was able to launch out into full-time ministry.

Many people are also encumbered with debts and other burdens. These things effectively keep people out of full-time ministry. Very few people are able to actually respond to the call of ministry.

If therefore you have been able to enter into full-time ministry, walk worthy of it because it was the grace of God that brought you in.

4. **It is more natural to live the life of an unbeliever than to serve God.**

So this I say, and affirm together with the Lord, that you WALK NO LONGER JUST AS THE GENTILES also walk, in the futility of their mind, being darkened in their understanding, excluded from the life of God because of the ignorance that is in them, because of the hardness of their heart;

Ephesians 4:17-18, NASB

The life of an unbeliever (a Gentile) follows a fixed pattern. Paul described this fixed pattern of living in Ephesians 4:17. There are three main characteristics of a Gentile's (unbeliever) life:

a. To live as an unbeliever is to walk in the futility of your mind.

Generally speaking, the life of an unbeliever is spent on futile and empty pursuits. It is a life of never-ending quests and useless ventures. Unbelievers spend their days building sandcastles, which are soon to be washed away by the sea. Everyone in full-time ministry could have spent his life chasing useless projects and imaginary goals. Sadly, the futility of all that men do is not obvious to them.

The heaping up of money, bank accounts and earthly treasures come to nothing but it is not easy to see. Most people never ask themselves why they are alive and why they are doing the things they do.

One day, a bank manager came to my house and left a complimentary card with the security man. When I woke up, the security man gave me the business card. As I studied this card, the Spirit said to me, "This lady is the manager of a sandcastle."

I was surprised at this statement coming from the Holy Spirit. But as I pondered over it, I realized that it was very very true. The bank is nothing but a sandcastle of imaginary wealth. It will perish and pass away with all its glory. I would rather be a door attendant in the permanent house of the Lord Jesus than to be the manager of a sandcastle organization.

The thinking of the Gentile mind is towards futility. Anybody who points out this futility looks strange. People would look at you strangely for calling the manager of a prestigious banking institution the manager of a sandcastle. In the world system, useless things are placed on a pedestal. They are feared and revered by one and all. It takes a man of the Spirit to see through the futility and the uselessness of it all. Surely, only a man of the Spirit can see and agree with the ancient Wisdom of Solomon: "...vanity of vanities; all is vanity" (Ecclesiastes 1:2).

b.   To live as an unbeliever is to be darkened in understanding.

The life of an unbeliever is lived out through his darkened (limited) understanding. Darkness imposes limitations on all activities. There are many things we cannot do in the night. Movement is restricted and most workplaces are closed. Nightfall and darkness therefore impose severe limitations on those experiencing it.

A Gentile, someone whose understanding is darkened, is therefore operating with a severely limited understanding. His thinking has been greatly reduced (darkened). He cannot see beyond this life.

Working in full-time ministry is only possible if limitations on your mind are lifted and you can see beyond this life. People in full-time ministry are seeing beyond this life. My eyes are fixed on eternal rewards.

I recently heard of how a very young executive of a billion dollar company died. It was sad because he was at the peak of his career. He had achieved many things older people could not achieve. However, he was struck with cancer and had to die sooner than he expected.

For whom shall be the things he had acquired? Where will they be stored? How long will they last? Will he be coming back to enjoy them? Will the people he left behind eat his millions while he is in the grave? Will his successors be wise or foolish? These are the questions someone with a darkened understanding is unable to answer. His mind is too limited to even think of these issues. These issues are too heavy for a darkened mind!

c. To live as an unbeliever is to be excluded from the life of God.

Unbelievers are excluded from the life of God. It is easy to exist on this earth without ever experiencing the life of God. Exclusion from the life of God is living without God's involvement and direction! You live by the uselessness of your own thinking.

You may create happiness in your myopic world but the absence of God in your life will lead to your eventual destruction.

Adam and Eve lived happily in the garden where God visited them. They had a job given to them by the Lord. After the incident with the tree of the knowledge of good and evil, they died and began to experience death. They were condemned to an existence of sweating and toiling for mere food. Their life was destroyed. They were no more living. They were existing and surviving to gather food for themselves. Life had lost its meaning because they were excluded from God.

Without the life of God, all your labour is to provide food, drink, clothing and shelter. With the life of God, you live for a higher purpose. You live to fulfil God's plan for your life. You live to obey His Word. That is the life of God!

The millionaires of this world do not know why they are alive. For whom do they labour? When will they get the chance to eat up all their treasures? Will they take these treasures away from this earth? What will happen to them when they die?

Exclusion from the life of God takes place because of ignorance of the Word. Born-again Christians must ensure they are not excluded from the life of God through ignorance. Constantly studying the Word of God will change you and bring you deeper into the life of God.

Throughout my years in ministry, I have learnt some things about handling God's privileges. Perhaps the most important thing to do in your privileged position is to walk worthily and carefully. God's grace must motivate you to walk worthily.

Don't Offer Strange Fire!

Live and conduct yourself carefully in this ministry. Nadab and Abihu are examples of priests who did not walk carefully in their calling. They died whilst walking in their calling of full-time ministry. They did not die because they were thieves or murderers. They died because they did not practise their ministry in the right way. They offered strange fire to the Lord. They did not walk worthy of their calling.

Now Nadab and Abihu, the sons of Aaron, took their respective firepans, and after putting fire in them, placed incense on it and offered strange fire before the LORD, which He had not commanded them.

AND FIRE CAME OUT FROM THE PRESENCE OF THE LORD AND CONSUMED THEM, and they died before the LORD. Then Moses said to Aaron, "It is what the LORD spoke, saying, 'By those who come near Me I will be treated as holy, And before all the people I will be honored'." So Aaron, therefore, kept silent.

Leviticus 10:1-3, NASB

We want to study how to offer God the kind of service and sacrifice He loves. We want to practise full-time ministry in a way that pleases God.

There are many Scriptures that exhort us to walk worthy of our calling. I was surprised to find that walking worthily involves developing important spiritual virtues like humility and patience. God's idea of how to walk worthy is probably different from yours. Notice these three Scriptures that exhort us to walk worthily in the ministry.

Therefore I, the prisoner of the Lord, implore you to WALK IN A MANNER WORTHY OF THE CALLING with which you have been called, with all humility and gentleness, with patience, showing tolerance for one another in love, being diligent to preserve the unity of the Spirit in the bond of peace.

Ephesians 4:1-3, NASB

So that you will WALK IN A MANNER WORTHY OF THE LORD, to please Him in all respects, bearing fruit in every good work and increasing in the knowledge of God; strengthened with all power, according to His glorious might, for the attaining of all steadfastness and patience; joyously

Colossians 1:10-11, NASB

Therefore, SINCE WE HAVE THIS MINISTRY, as we received mercy, WE DO not lose heart, but we have renounced the things hidden because of shame, not walking in craftiness or adulterating the word of

God, but by the manifestation of truth commending ourselves to every man's conscience in the sight of God.

2 Corinthians 4:1-2, NASB

Twenty Ways to Walk Worthy

1. Be humble in full-time ministry.

...walk in a manner worthy...with all humility...

Ephesians 4:1-2, NASB

The most important way of walking worthy is to walk in humility.

Recently, whilst writing a book, I had a revelation about a great ministry that had gone down from its former glory. The Lord showed me in a flash that those people had not walked in humility when their ministry grew. This church had publicly criticized other ministries and ridiculed ministers from their pulpit. At the peak of their ministry, they would ask people who came from other churches to stand up for cleansing (from the contamination of other ministries).

There are many ways to respond to God's promotion in ministry.

When the Lord gave Solomon the blessing of building a mega temple, he did not praise himself or think more highly of his achievements than he should. He actually demeaned his own achievements. He declared that the temple he had built was nothing. He knew that his great temple was simply a human attempt to do something for the Lord.

Notice the prayer of Solomon:

But will God indeed dwell on the earth? Behold, heaven and the highest heaven cannot contain You, how much less this house which I have built!

1 Kings 8:27, NASB

When you accomplish something for the Lord, you must see it in the right light. You have done nothing! God did not need you or me. It is His grace that makes it possible for us even to be around.

2. Gentleness in full-time ministry

...walk in a manner worthy...with gentleness...

Ephesians 4:1-2, NASB

To be gentle means to do things gradually. When you are in full-time ministry you must do things gradually. If you try to achieve certain heights in a hurry, you will have disaster. There are new ministers who want to be on television and radio in the first part of their ministry. Others want to write books because everyone is writing a book.

When you are not gentle, you push others around and you become frustrated about your apparent lack of success in the ministry.

3. Patience in full-time ministry

...walk in a manner worthy...with patience...

Ephesians 4:1-2, NASB

You must be patient in full-time ministry. You will not succeed overnight. Most of the casualties of full-time ministry were impatient. They could not wait to be bishops. They were not content with little things they were given to do. They wanted to hurry to the top. They drove faster and faster until there was a terrible accident.

4. Tolerance for one another in full-time ministry

...walk in a manner worthy...showing tolerance for one another...

Ephesians 4:1-2, NASB

It is necessary to be tolerant of others in the church. Working in a church involves working with others. You need to accept others as you work with them. Just like any other workplace, the church is full of human beings.

As soon as there is strife in the church, the anointing of the Lord is hindered. Let nothing be done through strife (Philippians 2:3). Full-time ministry must not be practiced through strife. Quarrels in the ministry should be treated as emergencies. They should be dealt with and the atmosphere of love must be maintained.

5.   Staying united in full-time ministry

...walk in a manner worthy...to preserve the unity of the Spirit...

Ephesians 4:1, 3 NASB

Staying united is very important to the Lord. Whatever you do in the church, do not create division. If you create divisions, you are not walking worthy of the privilege of ministry. There is one body and we will not allow anyone to divide us into groups based on tribe, nationality or any other idea.

6.   Ensure peace in full-time ministry.

...walk in a manner worthy...to preserve...the bond of peace.

Ephesians 4:1, 3 NASB

Peace is essential for building. King Solomon was able to build many things because he had peace. Solomon's armies were used for building instead of fighting. Any ministry which fights within itself will not build much for God.

7.   Please God in full-time ministry.

...walk in a manner worthy...to please Him...

Colossians 1:10, NASB

Surprisingly, not everybody in full-time ministry pleases the Lord. It is important to please God in whatever you do. Like Nadab and Abihu, God may be displeased with you even though you spend most of your time in the church. Endeavour to please God even in full-time ministry. For instance, I know of only one thing that causes a stir in Heaven - soul winning. When you win a soul, you make the Father happy. Soul winning is one of the many activities a full-time minister can pursue. I assure you, it is one thing that will please the Father.

8. Be fruitful in full-time ministry.

...walk in a manner worthy...bearing fruit...
Colossians 1:10, NASB

There are differences in employees. Some members of staff are very fruitful and contribute greatly to the efforts of the ministry. Others are more of a burden. Ensure that you are one of those whose presence is beneficial to the work of God. The fact that you are paid by the organization does not mean that you are fruitful.

9. Increase in the knowledge of God in full-time ministry.

...walk in a manner worthy...increasing in the knowledge of God;
Colossians 1:10

One interesting phenomenon is that some people actually backslide when they are in full-time ministry. They actually pray less and read less than when they were lay people. The fact that you work in a church does not mean that you will be automatically full of the Word. Endeavour to increase in the knowledge of God even as you serve God in full-time ministry.

10. Become stronger spiritually.

...walk in a manner worthy...strengthened...
Colossians 1:10-11, NASB

You must become stronger spiritually now that you are in full-time ministry. Pray more and wait on the Lord. God will bless you.

11. Be steadfast in full-time ministry.

...walk in a manner worthy...attaining...all steadfastness...

Colossians 1:10-11, NASB

You must be steady and unmovable in the ministry. Financial pressures and job offers must not be able to move you away from your calling. As you work in full-time ministry, you will attain steadfastness. Steadfastness is the ability to stay on course. Steadfastness is also the ability to come back to the course when you drift away. Do not drift from full-time ministry. There are many things to drift into. Business, education, relief work, social work, etc., are common roads that full-time ministers drift into.

12. Become happy in full-time ministry.

...walk in a manner worthy...joyously

Colossians 1:10-11, NASB

Full-time ministry is a joyful time. You must have a joyful attitude in ministry. Working in the ministry is better than working in the bank. Full-time ministry is better than working in the hospital. People who have tasted working for the Lord will not want to go back to the world.

13. Be thankful that you are in full-time ministry.

...walk in a manner worthy...giving thanks...

Colossians 1:10,12 NASB

Your heart must be full of thanks everyday for the great opportunity that God has given you to work for Him. If you are not thankful, you are probably in the wrong place. The more time you spend working in the ministry, the more thankful you should become.

14. Do not lose heart in full-time ministry.

...since we have this ministry...we do not lose heart

2 Corinthians 4:1-2, NASB

Ministry is not easy. There are many things that can discourage you. Much of what you do is hard work, with no one appreciating your efforts. You are working for the Lord and not for any man. It is when you look to people for appreciation that you become discouraged.

15. Renounce hidden things of dishonesty.

...since we have this ministry...we have renounced the things hidden because of shame...
2 Corinthians 4:1-2, NASB

Dishonest people cannot flourish in ministry. The reason is that the boss (God) has His eyes everywhere. Unlike other jobs where you can get away with stealing and other dishonest practices, you cannot steal from God.

There are people who think they have duped the Lord but no one can hoodwink the King of Kings.

16. Do not be crafty.

Since we have this ministry...not walking in craftiness
2 Corinthians 4:1-2, NASB

Craftiness speaks of being cleverly able to cut corners and get away with poor work. Unfortunately, this is not possible with Jehovah. Leave your crooked ways behind and let us work for the Lord without craftiness.

17. Do not adulterate the Word of God.

...since we have this ministry...not...adulterating the word of God...
2 Corinthians 4:1-2, NASB

The Word of God cannot be tampered with. Many people have tried to water down His precious Gospel. They have sought to re-present the Gospel as some kind of good advice for successful living. We cannot do anything that will destroy the truth of God's work. Do not change His Word; just preach it as it is.

18. Commend yourself to the conscience of men.

...since we have this ministry...commending ourselves to every man's conscience...

2 Corinthians 4:1-2, NASB

It is important to commend yourself to men's consciences. Often they will criticize you but in their hearts they respect what you are doing.

19. Commend yourself to men in God's sight.

...since we have this ministry...commending ourselves to every man's conscience in the sight of God.

2 Corinthians 4:1-2, NASB

All that we do must have approval in the sight of God. No human being or human institution can declare our work approved or disapproved. It is time to think only of what God says.

20. Make sure the Gospel is not hidden because of us.

And even if our gospel is veiled, it is veiled to those who are perishing, in whose case the god of this world has blinded the minds of the unbelieving so that they might not see the light of the gospel of the glory of Christ, who is the image of God.

2 Corinthians 4:3-4, NASB

Finally, the aim of full-time ministry is to ensure that the Gospel is known and heard in every corner of the world. How unfortunate it is that many people do not hear the Gospel.

All the efforts and money of the modern church must be directed to ensure that the Gospel is not hidden even from the remotest village. The Gospel must not be hidden from the poor. The way we operate the ministry must ensure that the Gospel is not hidden from anyone.

Chapter 4

Ten Types of Workers

1. Workers who are sons and daughters

But ye know the proof of him, that, AS A SON WITH THE FATHER, he hath served with me in the gospel.

Philippians 2:22

There are people who work in the ministry as sons and daughters of the ministry. Such people live and work as though they are in a family business. They do not have the usual employee attitude. They are more of family members. Also, such people do not have the usual "I am here for what I can get" attitude.

I find that many difficulties are eliminated by working with sons and daughters. You will probably enjoy working with your father more than with your boss!

In reality, not all workers in full-time ministry are sons or daughters of the ministry. Some are simply good people who want to work for God.

2. Workers who have the same spirit as the leader

I desired Titus, and with him I sent a brother. Did Titus make a gain of you? walked we not in THE SAME SPIRIT? walked we not in the same steps?

2 Corinthians 12:18

There are people who work in the ministry but have a different spirit from their leader. It is a blessing to find people who work with you with "the same spirit".

Paul was not in the ministry for financial gain and he found in Titus someone with the same spirit. You do not need to stay long in the ministry to find out that people work in the ministry for different reasons. What a blessing it is to find someone who will work with you in the ministry with the same spirit!

3. Workers who work for you because they owe their whole life to you

I Paul have written it with mine own hand, I will repay it: albeit I do not say to thee how thou OWEST UNTO ME EVEN THINE OWN SELF besides.

Philemon 1:19

There are people who work in the ministry out of a sense of gratitude and indebtedness to God. Such people are often grateful for their salvation and feel that they owe their lives to you.

If people really understood what their salvation was, they would spend the rest of their days in full-time service to God. Seventy years of working for God would not be able to pay for the blessing of salvation.

4. Workers who are prone to abandoning you

For DEMAS HATH FORSAKEN me, having loved this present world, and is departed unto Thessalonica; Crescens to Galatia, Titus unto Dalmatia.

2 Timothy 4:10

Every ministry has a "Demas". Demas is the minister or employee who abandons ship in the midst of the journey. Do not become the Demas of your church and ministry.

There are people who are given to you for life. God has called some of us to live and work together for the rest of our lives. There is a feeling of peace as you work with this permanent family.

Sadly, there is a type of full-time minister who will abandon you midstream. After being in the ministry for some time, I can often see the type of person who will suddenly resign from the ministry.

5. Workers who refresh you

The Lord give mercy unto the house of Onesiphorus; for HE OFT REFRESHED ME, and was not ashamed of my chain:

2 Timothy 1:16

The most refreshing people are those who are not ashamed of you. They love everything about you, including the unattractive parts. It is only the deepest kind of love that embraces everything; the good, the bad and the ugly.

Such people are not serving you for money. They are there because of a very personal love for the leader. I always sense when people have a personal love for me. I also sense when they know I am not perfect but they still love me.

Every minister has a shameful chain around him. Not everyone who works in the ministry has this personal and permanent love. May you have the spirit of Onesiphorus. May you bring refreshing to the man God has called you to.

6. Workers who are servants of the church.

I commend unto you Phebe our sister, which is A SERVANT OF THE CHURCH which is at Cenchrea:

Romans 16:1

There are people who bestow much service on the church in general. They are a blessing to many people. The impact of the servants of the church is seen best when they die. I have never forgotten the different people who have served me through the years.

Some have made themselves into errand boys and girls. They have served and helped in almost every imaginable capacity. I know that God will bless them on the Day of Judgement.

Although most church members' deaths would go unnoticed, the whole church feels the loss of the Phebes of the ministry. Phebe, without using the pulpit, touched the lives of many people.

7. Couples who are in full-time ministry together

Greet Priscilla and Aquila my helpers in Christ Jesus:

Romans 16:3

It is a special privilege for a man of God to have both husband and wife working together to help him. What a blessing it is for the whole family to work together in full-time ministry.

It is a special blessing for couples to both find a place in the house of God. Couples in ministry have a more synchronized lifestyle that may enhance their relationship.

Many full-time ministers take Mondays as their day off. However, in the secular world, Monday is the first and most important day of the week. This difference in schedules can separate couples who do not work together in the ministry.

In addition, a spouse who does not work in the ministry often despises the one in full-time ministry. They think their spouses are wasting their time by working for a church. They do not respect the ministry and therefore they do not respect people who work full-time in it.

These people also do not understand what could make someone busy in the church. Because the secular spouse despises full-time ministry he often sends the full-time spouse on domestic errands. Sadly, such people see the spouse in full-time ministry as unemployed.

There are also disadvantages of couples working in the same place, but the advantages outweigh the disadvantages.

8. Hard-working workers

Greet Mary, who bestowed MUCH LABOUR on us.

Romans 16:6

There are always the workhorses of ministry. Ministry involves a lot of hard work and there are always people who take on the burden of the work. They bestow much labour and exert much effort to accomplish ministry tasks.

This is what Paul meant when he spoke of Mary who worked so hard when he visited. God sees all the hard work that everyone puts into the ministry and He will reward it.

In His letter to the Ephesian church, the Lord made special mention of the labours and the hard work of the church. God notices hard work!

I know thy works, and thy labour, and thy patience, and how thou canst not bear them which are evil... And hast borne, and hast patience, and for my name's sake hast laboured, and hast not fainted.

Revelation 2:2-3

9. Workers who are women and cannot stop quarrelling

I beseech Euodias, and beseech Syntyche, that they be of the same mind in the Lord

Philippians 4:2

Women are most precious workers who love the Lord with all their heart and with all their feelings. One of the side effects of ladies working together is female bickering and quarrelling.

Paul found himself in the middle of female quarrelling and had to dedicate part of his church letter to solving a problem between two ladies.

Some of these quarrels and cold wars may be inevitable when women work together. God wants women to work for Him and they have a valuable contribution to make!

As we mature in the love of God, the Euodias-Syntyche syndrome will surely manifest! But the love of God will smoothen out all these things.

10. Full-time apostles

Salute Andronicus and Junia, my kinsmen, and my fellow prisoners, who are of note among the apostles, who also were in Christ before me.

Romans 16:7

The work of the apostle is to create something that did not exist. There are some workers who can make something out of nothing. You can send them on a mission and they will bulldoze their way through all obstacles, accomplishing and creating as they go along.

In every ministry, there are people whose contribution is of special note. After the apostle has built the church, every other ministry has something to do. Truly, the apostles are noteworthy among the team of full-time workers.

Beginning a ministry is very difficult. It takes determination, faith and resilience to pull through with a pioneering work. We must respect the grace of God that is upon apostles amongst us who are able to begin things that stand the test of time.

Chapter 5

The Ten Laws of Your Mission

Working in the ministry is working for Christ Jesus. He has given us guidelines for the accomplishment of His mission. When He commissioned His apostles, He said many things which were intended to guide them in full-time ministry. These instructions can be called the "Laws of the Mission" since they serve as a guide on how to behave during the mission. I want us to go through several of these Laws of the Mission.

1. The law of knowing your calling

For ye see your calling, brethren, how that not many wise men after the flesh, not many mighty, not many noble, are called:

1 Corinthians 1:26

It is important to know your particular calling. Most people do not know what their calling is. As you serve the Lord, you will see things which help reveal your particular call. The Bible teaches that you see and know things about your calling.

For ye see your calling, brethren, how that...

1 Corinthians 1:26

It is important to discover a lot about your calling and to know what it actually involves.

But go rather to the lost sheep of the house of Israel.

Matthew 10:6

The disciples were called specifically to the house of Israel. Their call was to Israel and not to the Gentiles. If Jesus had not specifically told them to go to the lost sheep of Israel, with time the apostles would have noticed that their calling was to Israel.

For instance, they could have recognized a stronger anointing and more success when they ministered to the lost sheep of

33

Israel. Perhaps they would have recognized how nothing worked when they tried ministering to Gentiles and Samaritans! They would soon have seen their calling; how that not many Gentiles or Samaritans were included in their ministry.

That is how you discover your calling. You watch what works. You observe what the Lord does with you and with your life. Then you begin to see and understand your calling. If you think you will have explicit details about your calling in a voice thundering from Heaven, you will probably wait forever. You have to watch your calling and flow with what God is doing.

2. The law of concentration and perfection

These twelve Jesus sent forth, and commanded them, saying, Go not into the way of the Gentiles, and into any city of the Samaritans enter ye not:
Matthew 10:5

In this law, Jesus teaches us to concentrate on our particular area of calling. In full-time ministry, we will only find true fruitfulness when we stay within the domain assigned to us.

Jesus told the Apostles to avoid Gentiles and Samaritans and concentrate on the lost sheep of Israel. When you know your calling, it is your duty to concentrate your efforts on your area of calling. As you do this you will become a better minister. People will recognize your gift in that area. This so-called gift is actually the fruit of you concentrating to perfect your calling.

3. The law of trusting God for finances

Provide neither gold, nor silver, nor brass in your purses, Nor scrip for your journey, neither two coats, neither shoes, nor yet staves: for the workman is worthy of his meat.
Matthew 10:9-10

Full-time ministry is all about trusting God for finances. Full-time ministry is not an alternative to your secular employment. Neither is it a place to achieve your financial aspirations.

It is all about trusting God for everything. God will take care of you as you work for Him. I cannot overemphasize this reality of ministry. Ministry is not for money. Ministry is for the service of God.

Anyone who does this sacred work with the intention of using the ministry as a source of riches is likely to end up in trouble. As old-fashioned as it may sound, you are going to have to trust God to provide everything for you.

4. The law of flexibility

And if the house be worthy, let your peace come upon it: but if it be not worthy, let your peace return to you. And whosoever shall not receive you, nor hear your words, when ye depart out of that house or city, shake off the dust of your feet.

Matthew 10:13-14

In ministry, you must be flexible and allow God to lead you in several different directions. It is good to start out trusting Him, but you must continue to be pliable in His hands. You must not be fixated to any particular role.

Sometimes, when something is not working, it is a sign that you must change direction. The Lord sent the disciples into the different cities. Some of these missions were doomed to fail but Jesus still asked them to go. However, He also told them to pack and leave immediately if the mission did not work.

Be ready to change course. Leave all options open. Be flexible and flow until you find your life's work!

5. The law of "absolute disconnection" from those who do not receive us nor believe in us

And whosoever shall not receive you, nor hear your words, when ye depart out of that house or city, shake off the dust of your feet.

Matthew 10:14

Not everybody is going to believe in your calling. There is no need to struggle with people who have reservations about what you are doing. Make new friends and stay with like-minded people. Avoid people who mock you. Blessed is the man that does not hang around mockers and scoffers.

There are people who consider full-time ministry to be madness of the highest order. There are born-again, Spirit-filled Christians who think that working in a church is for the elderly or emotionally unstable. Becoming a missionary is seen as something for people without a successful career.

6. The law of "snake wisdom"

Behold, I send you forth as sheep in the midst of wolves: be ye therefore wise as serpents, and harmless as doves.

Matthew 10:16

This law speaks of the importance and wisdom of privacy, confidentiality, and secrecy in ministry. It is fatally deficient wisdom to expose all that you are and all that you have to everyone. Once you are in the ministry, never believe that the world loves or accepts you. Assume that you are disliked, disbelieved, disregarded and disrespected by the world, its journalists and its politicians. We have been sent forth as sheep in the midst of wolves.

7. The law of wariness of men

But beware of men: for they will deliver you up to the councils, and they will scourge you in their synagogues;

Matthew 10:17

"Beware of men" are the words of Jesus to His disciples. He did not even say we should beware of devils. More harm can come to a minister through men than you imagine. A minister who makes close friends of worldly politicians and journalists may be setting himself up for an unpleasant experience.

Pastors are simply not respected by worldly business people and bank managers. Many of these businessmen see ministers as crooks. They just humour us and put up with us because they have to and because we sometimes give them good business. Beware of people who do not love you! Beware of men!

8. The law of the free Gospel

...freely ye have received, freely give.

Matthew 10:8

The Gospel was brought to us at no charge. We must endeavour to give it back freely. In order to give freely there are many things full-time workers must be conscious of.

We must reduce the cost of running the ministry. The cost of equipment, electricity, buildings, etc. must be brought to a minimum if we are to make the Gospel free. Our salaries also must be as low as possible. Does the ministry take care of our needs or does the ministry spend its money supporting our lifestyles?

9. The law of avoiding internal fighting

And he called them unto him, and said unto them in parables, How can Satan cast out Satan?

Mark 3:23

We stand no chance if we fight each other internally. There are some common but secret fights that go on in many churches and ministries. In the secret places of ministry, pastors often fight against other pastors.

Another internal but secret fight that goes on in the ministry is the fight between husbands and wives.

Yet another internal battle goes on amongst women who are jealous of each other. These battles are real and sometimes very bloody. Do not be surprised if you find yourself embroiled in one of these fights. But the warning is stern. We stand no chance against the real enemy if we exert our energies against one another!

10. The law of rewards

There is a reward for the smallest job in full-time ministry. Do not be discouraged if the work you do looks insignificant. In Heaven, you will be rewarded for your faithfulness to what you were given! I do not know what job you do, but I am sure it is more noteworthy than serving a glass of water. Is it not encouraging to know that even serving a glass of water will be rewarded in Heaven?

And whosoever shall give to drink unto one of these little ones a cup of cold water only in the name of a disciple, verily I say unto you, he shall in no wise lose his reward.

Matthew 10:42

Chapter 6

How to be a Good
Personal Assistant

...who had ability for serving in the king's court...

Daniel 1:4, NASB

A s you set out to serve God in the ministry you may find
yourself serving a man of God. Actually, the ministry is not
about working in an institution but about serving an anointed man
of God. Serving in the ministry is very different from working
in the bank.

Not everyone will have the opportunity to work directly for the
anointed man of God. Maybe, one day, you will have a chance to
minister to God's servant personally. There are some things that
are important for every full-time worker to know about becoming
a personal servant to the man of God.

1. Accept the personal choices of the man of God.

**And he goeth up into a mountain, and calleth unto him
WHOM HE WOULD: and they came unto him.**

Mark 3:13

Jesus chose whom He would. It was His personal decision. It
was His preference. No one could choose His disciples for Him.
Every leader has a right to choose those he wants to be with him.

God has designed us to make choices. Obviously, the leader
cannot have everyone close to him.

Do not be angry if you are not chosen. Some people will be
privileged and chosen to serve in the "king's court". This is a
special calling. Do not fight the leader's choices. The leader
will like you if you like his choice and will reject you if you
reject his choice.

2. Accept the values of the man of God.

Every leader has personal needs. It is sometimes difficult to understand the needs and idiosyncrasies of some leaders. Depending on the needs a leader has, certain things will be important to him. The ability of someone to satisfy any of the special needs of the leader makes a person very valuable. Sometimes the value a leader places on the helper who meets his special needs may seem disproportionate to the importance ascribed to the person. You may not understand why the leader fusses over someone until you find yourself in his shoes.

Hiring a special singer or an organist may not seem important to some. For instance, a good singer may be worth millions to a ministering prophet.

Similarly, things that do not look valuable to us may be very valuable to God. You may be the most valuable person to God because you do something that your heavenly Father really loves.

3. Accept the man of God's need for genuine friends.

Every king needs friends, every king wants friends and every king has friends! If you can be the friend of the leader, you will be valuable to him.

King David's friend was Hushai the Archite (2 Samuel 15:37) and King Solomon's friend was Zabud (1 Kings 4:5). Jesus' friends were Lazarus, Martha and Mary, her sister.

Now Jesus loved Martha, and her sister, and Lazarus.

John 11:5

Every leader is still a human being and as such needs people to talk to. He needs people he can be relaxed with.

You can't be serious all the time; saying the right things, always behaving like the United Nations Secretary General on a diplomatic mission!

You need people with whom you can be relaxed and who are at ease around you. Somehow, not everyone can be relaxed in the presence of a king.

Also, most people cannot comprehend that they can have a down-to-earth friendship and relationship with the king. More and more, I realize that not everyone can serve in the king's court!

Shadrach, Meshach and Abednego were people who had, amongst other things, the ability to serve in the king's court. They had the special grace to hang around the king's environs and to relate with all that went on there.

Youths in whom was no defect, who were good-looking, showing intelligence in every branch of wisdom, endowed with understanding and discerning knowledge, and who had ABILITY FOR SERVING IN THE KING'S COURT...

Daniel 1:4, NASB

A wise king knows that he is often surrounded by liars, thieves, treacherous people, wicked men, accusers, fault- finders and many poor and hungry-eyed men, looking for what they can get!

Oh, how he wishes for a few moments of respite, where he can be relaxed without fear. Perhaps it is in this that the friend finds his highest value! Someone with whom the leader can be at ease!

4. Accept the humble duties of a personal assistant.

There are servants who meet the personal needs of the leader. These personal servants may be demeaned in the eyes of onlookers.

Joshua was a personal servant of Moses but he became the leader of Israel. Elisha was the personal servant of Elijah and he received a double portion of the anointing.

Becoming a personal servant may be your door to the anointing! Indeed it is a privilege to pour water on the hands of the man of God, because very few people will ever have the opportunity to do that.

Verily, verily, I say unto you, He that receiveth whomsoever I send receiveth me; and he that receiveth me receiveth him that sent me.

John 13:20

5. Accept the spiritual opportunities that come with personal service.

And he ordained twelve, that they should BE WITH HIM, and that he might send them forth to preach,

Mark 3:14

The Lord did not take on the disciples for any particular job. He took them on so that they would be with Him.

There are many people that I employ just so that they will be near me. After being around the anointing for some time, people are ready to be sent.

Personal servants thus go through two phases of ministry. The first phase is the *"be with me"* phase. The second phase is the *"sending out"* phase.

6. Understand the dangers of familiarity in personal service.

For neither did his brethren believe in him.

John 7:5

Personal servants can easily become familiar. Through familiarity, Jesus' own family did not believe in him.

When you see the human side of God's servant, you can be tempted to think you are not dealing with the power of God. Perhaps this is what happened to Judas. All personal servants must be careful of becoming another Judas. Beware of familiarity.

7. Avoid the dangers of being unspiritual around a spiritual person.

...Martha, Martha, thou art careful and troubled about many things: But one thing is needful: and MARY HATH CHOSEN THAT GOOD PART, which shall not be taken away from her.

Luke 10:41-42

When you are involved in personal service, make sure you get the "good part". The *good part* of personal ministry is not the physical advantage, but the spiritual treasure. Unfortunately, many people who work closely and personally with a man of God miss the spiritual treasures of close fellowship.

The book of John reveals the treasures experienced when Jesus interacted personally and privately with His disciples.

The things He said were not for public consumption. They would never be heard by the crowds but they would be heard by the few around Him.

Martha was very close to Jesus but Jesus was not happy with her spirituality. He would have preferred it if she was more interested in the Word of God. *Every personal servant must be careful of being unspiritual around a spiritual person.*

Jesus knew that the job of serving food would be taken away from Martha. But the spiritual treasures that Mary was receiving were eternal. It is interesting to note that Jesus was still friendly to Martha even though she was not interested in the Word. Jesus still liked her very much and He enjoyed her food.

The fact that the spiritual leader likes you does not mean that you will do well on the Day of Judgement.

This is a common delusion for those in the personal company of spiritual leaders. They have the greatest privilege to be close but are in great danger of being unaffected by the anointing and the Word.

8. Accept the opportunity to become part of a new family.

Christ's disciples were one big family. This family spirit often develops as several people work in the personal service of the apostle.

Jesus called the people who worked with Him, His "mother" and His "brothers". This must be the pattern for all followers of Christ. Create a family out of your full-time staff! Let them be your brothers, mothers and sisters.

And he answered them, saying, WHO IS MY MOTHER, OR MY BRETHREN? And he looked round about on them which sat about him, and said, Behold my mother and my brethren!
For whosoever shall do the will of God, the same is my brother, and my sister, and mother.

Mark 3:33-35

A family spirit can be nurtured in every workplace. This family spirit is even more important for growth in the ministry.

Chapter 7

The Laws of Placement

Everybody wants to be at the top and everybody wants to have the best possible job. Somehow, everybody must be placed in the most suitable position. So how do we get to the best places and what is the reason for being put in certain positions?

There are spiritual laws that govern where you must be placed in the ministry. In this chapter I want you to look at some of these laws so that you will have the understanding and the humility that is necessary to function effectively.

1. The law of "those who came first"

...After me comes a Man who has a higher rank than I, for He existed before me.

John 1:30, NASB

This law teaches that those who come first are senior to those who come later. John the Baptist indicated that he had a senior in the ministry - Jesus Christ. He explained that Jesus was there before he was. In a spiritual sense, Jesus existed before John the Baptist. That is why Jesus was greater than he was.

2. The law of personal preference

This is another law that determines where you will be placed in the ministry. The "law of personal preference" can override the law of "those who came first". Generally speaking, the law of "who came first" usually applies.

Sometimes, someone who is a late entrant may be given a higher rank. This is because there may be other factors that necessitate a newcomer having a higher rank.

John came onto the ministry scene before Jesus. Yet Jesus was given a higher rank than him.

> **After me comes a Man who has a higher rank than I, for He existed before me.**
>
> **John 1:30, NASB**

Other Scriptures testify to the reality that God has a personal choice and He exercises it as He wills. God's election can override the law of "who came first".

> **For the children being not yet born, neither having done any good or evil, that the purpose of God according to election might stand, not of works, but of him that calleth. It was said unto her, The elder shall serve the younger. As it is written, Jacob have I loved, but Esau have I hated. What shall we say then? Is there unrighteousness with God? God forbid. For he saith to Moses, I will have mercy on whom I will have mercy, and I will have compassion on whom I will have compassion. So then it is not of him that willeth, nor of him that runneth, but of God that sheweth mercy.**
>
> **Romans 9:11-16**

3. The law of militarized work

> **No man that warreth entangleth himself with the affairs of this life...**
>
> **2 Timothy 2:4**

In full-time ministry, you cannot determine where you will be placed or where you will live. This is the reason why there are no guarantees and no securities in full-time ministry. The law of militarized work tells us that you can be sent anywhere at any time.

When you work in a militarized environment expect changes at any time. When you are in the army, you can be sent to your death at any time. Militarized work has no working hours. Militarized work is hard and full of risks. Many people die doing militarized work. You must have a militarized attitude in the ministry. Be ready to be sent anywhere or to be placed anywhere. Be ready to die for the cause when you are called upon.

4. The law of spiritual intimacy in ministry

Seemeth it but a small thing unto you, that the God of Israel hath separated you from the congregation of Israel, to bring you near to himself to do the service of the tabernacle of the LORD, and to stand before the congregation to minister unto them?

Numbers 16:9

The most important place for you is to be close to the Lord. Instead of seeking to be placed in seemingly prestigious positions, seek to be placed close to the Lord. Whether you are on the top floor or underground, aim to be close to the Lord.

Get this! Full-time ministry is intended to bring you close to the Lord; to make you an intimate friend of Jesus! God's intention for you in full-time ministry is to bring you close to Himself.

Notice what Moses told Korah. He pointed out that Korah had been brought near to do the service.

Spirituality and intimacy are choices you must make for yourself in full-time ministry.

5. The law of the candlestick position

This law teaches that love and intimacy will guarantee your position in the presence of the Lord. Everyone has a candlestick and your candlestick will be moved from where it is if you depart from love and intimacy with the Lord!

Hard work is no substitute for love and intimacy. God wants people to come close to Him. If we seek Him, we will find Him. In the book of Revelation, there was a church that worked harder than any other did. However, the Lord was not pleased with them. Hard work is not a substitute for a loving and intimate relationship. On two different occasions the Lord said to the church,

I know your labor." He knew they were a hard-working group.

He said to them:

I know thy works, and thy labour, and thy patience, and how thou canst not bear them which are evil: and thou hast tried them which say they are apostles, and are not, and hast found them liars:

And hast borne, and hast patience, and for my name's sake hast laboured, and hast not fainted. Nevertheless I have somewhat against thee, because thou hast left thy first love.

Revelation 2:2-4

They were indeed a labouring and toiling church but they were not intimate with the Lord. Because of this, they were in danger of being removed from their position. He warned them, "I will come and remove your candlestick out of its place."

6. The law of increasing goods

When goods increase, they are increased that eat them: and what good is there to the owners thereof, saving the beholding of them with their eyes?

Ecclesiastes 5:11

This law teaches that no matter where you are placed or what you earn, there will be things to swallow up your earnings.

Many workers are deluded into thinking that if they had a better position and earned more money they would be better off. But this is simply not the case.

As money increases, there are more things to do with the money. It is this delusion that drives people to attain certain positions. It is this delusion that makes workers dissatisfied with where they are placed.

Discover the secret of contentment. Believe that God rules in your affairs. You can be blessed in every position and in every circumstance.

Chapter 8

How Your Value Is Determined

Determining the value of anything is not easy. People go to the university for years to study "valuation". What is the value of a house? What is the value of a car? What is the value of a person? What is the value of a person to God? Obviously, the values of things change from person to person. Someone may value a diamond whilst another may kick it away as a worthless stone.

When you work for the Lord, you must seek to increase your value! You must understand what makes you valuable and do those things. You must understand what valuable thing God has placed in you and develop it.

Several things determine your value. Different people value different things. It is important to know some of the different things that increase or decrease your *personal* value.

How to Increase Your Value

1. Your value increases when you can be sent.

...Here am I; send me.

Isaiah 6:8

Not everyone is sendable. A person being sent on a mission must have the special ability to be faithful without varying the message. Most people who are sent on a mission become sympathetic to the people they are sent to and modify their mission and their message!

If you look closely at the church today, you will find a modified message with a modified mission. I once sent somebody on a very simple mission. After a while, I realized that the person had become sympathetic to the group I had sent him to. This individual fell in love with the group and wanted me to support them financially. He constantly referred to the needs of the group rather than the message I had sent him with.

Once, without my knowledge, this person pledged my financial support to things I had not intended to do. After a while, I realized that I was sending the wrong person. My messenger had become sympathetic to the people he had been sent to. O how valuable it is to have someone you can send!

Someone who will not change the message! Someone whose heart will not change with time! Someone who will stay with the mission. Thank God for those who can stay with the message no matter how hard or ridiculous it sounds.

2. Your value increases when you can bring projects to a close.

To the inexperienced, this point may seem even frivolous. But I have employed different people, assigned them to various projects, and found them unable to conclude just the final little part.

Some people are able to start projects and carry them for a good distance. Amazingly, they are not able to conclude on their project even though they have come ninety per cent of the way. The last ten per cent of every project is a crucial final piece.

Hope deferred makes the heart sick; when the hope of accomplished tasks is dashed repeatedly, the heart of the leader is sickened.

A beautiful car, without one of its tyres, is the same as not having a car because a car with three tyres cannot be driven. Many people do not realize that one little uncompleted segment neutralizes everything else.

Jesus is the author and finisher of our faith. Some people are authors of things but not finishers. Your value greatly multiplies when you can finish what you have begun.

Every task has a whole lot of problems that will prevent its conclusion. Some people who are sent are unable to find solutions to these problems. They simply report back with their list of insurmountable problems.

However, the finisher will break through the barriers and overcome every obstacle. Such people are truly valuable. They just come home with a list of victories. They tell you how they overcame the different obstacles they encountered.

3. Your value increases when you can accomplish tasks with speed.

It is a pleasure to have a fast and reliable worker. I have had workers who accomplish tasks at different speeds. I prefer to work with people who bring projects to a close quickly. In fact, the value of someone who can rapidly conclude projects is very high.

I place a high premium on speed because delays are expensive and often lead to the cancellation of the original vision.

4. Your value increases with your ability to solve diverse problems.

There are people who can solve diverse problems and bulldoze their way through obstacles. I have people on my staff like that. They can deal with all kinds of people and solve all kinds of problems.

Whether the issues are private or public, they are able to sort them out. They can deal with difficult people, manage crises, help with personal matters and defeat the enemy. Such people are very valuable because life is full of diverse problems. Problems do not come in departments or under any particular headings. You need people who can solve problems no matter the category they fall into.

5. Your value is greater if you are involved in building a foundation.

You are those who have stood by Me in My trials; and just as My Father has granted Me a kingdom, I grant you that you may eat and drink at My table in My

kingdom, and you will sit on thrones judging the twelve tribes of Israel.

Luke 22:28-30, NASB

The foundation of a building is the most difficult part to build. There are always some people who help to set things up. The contribution of such people is priceless. These people must never be forgotten. They are to be treasured and valued above those who come later. Anyone who wishes to set them aside does not understand what he is doing.

Jesus Himself promised His disciples that He would remember them especially because they had been with Him during the most trying times of His ministry.

Foundation builders suffer things that future workers will never experience. They experience the greatest pressures of the ministry. There are pastors who can build large churches but cannot actually begin one. Do not shy away from starting things. It may be your great opportunity to become valuable.

6. Your value increases with your ability to keep secrets.

No king would like to have a blabbermouth by his side. Many confidential things go on in the king's palace. Keeping things private and confidential may be one of the most important things to do. Anyone who works in the office of leadership must learn the importance of privacy and secrecy. Unfortunately, some people do not have the ability to work without talking about what they do.

Working in banks requires lots of secrecy because you deal with people's private wealth; one who cannot keep official information out of his domestic chatter will be unsuitable for such a job. Upon employment, banks will make you sign the oath of secrecy.

Working in a pastor's office may involve listening to private counselling sessions. Working in a doctor's office may also involve hearing and seeing people's personal problems. These private matters are nobody's business and should not be broadcast to the world. No one would like the whole world to know his personal problems.

Your value increases when you prove that you are capable of handling the responsibility of secrets. Some people will be employed simply because they do not have many friends! Some people will get certain jobs because they do not talk much with anyone about anything!

For this kind of job, you will have to avoid people who talk too much and have too many friends!

These "talkative" people will become valuable for the office party and other social gatherings where they will bring everything to life. Please understand what makes you valuable.

7. Your value increases when you are "good" company.

And he ordained twelve, THAT THEY SHOULD BE WITH HIM.

Mark 3:14

Jesus ordained twelve disciples simply so they would be with Him. He chose them to be in His company until He finished His ministry.

Not everybody can work comfortably with the boss. To work directly with the boss requires varied skills. The commander requires people who can engage in interesting and meaningful conversation. Some people just have nothing to say and therefore are not good company.

The Silent Hungry Look

Quiet people can be intolerable for a wise leader, as he has to constantly pry into their minds to find out what they are thinking.

His wisdom will cause him to search out hidden thoughts in case there are evolving plots against his life.

When I am with "quiet" people I always ask, "What do you think?" "How is your mind working? Is it a good idea?" I want to know what people around me are thinking.

Julius Caesar commented on Cassius, a worker in his court.

He said, "Yon Cassius has a lean and hungry look. He thinks too much: such men are dangerous."

Cassius was one of the conspirators who murdered Caesar. Long before the assassination, Caesar mistrusted Cassius because of the silent, hungry look on his face.

The Empty Look

Others only enjoy talking about light and frivolous matters, which may not interest the leader. Leaders are not light-hearted men of straw. They are serious people who have serious issues to deal with.

Rulers have many issues to juggle with and value people who are full of good counsel and wisdom. Leadership is a very lonely job with few who understand the real issues and challenges at hand. Many people simply see the leader as a superman who knows everything and who is always right. Such an attitude will not go well with a leader who wants the input of those around him. He therefore needs people who think and analyze issues in a certain way.

The Suspicious Look

A leader is someone who fights many battles. He does not need a cabinet member who is suspicious and opposed to all he does. This only transfers the battle from outside to within. Why should you employ someone to oppose and resist you?

Leaders also need people who think in a certain way. Paul said of Timothy,

> **...I have no man likeminded, who will naturally care for your state.**
>
> **Philippians 2:20**

King David had Hushai as his friend and King Solomon had Zabud as a friend. These friends were good company, good fellowship and gave good counsel.

The Creative Look

Creativity is the nature of God. People who are innovative and come up with good ideas when they are needed are also very valuable company.

Another important and valuable trait is the ability to meet the personal needs of the leader. Not everyone can work comfortably in the personal service of the king. Daniel and his three friends had the ability to serve in the king's court. This, too, is an important skill.

> **...bring in some of the sons of Israel...who had ability for serving in the king's court...they were to enter the king's personal service.**
>
> **Daniel 1:3-5, NASB**

8. Your value increases when you can relate well with outsiders.

There are people who can relate easily with the outside world. However, not all workers are up to this role.

To effectively relate with outsiders, you need to develop the art of diplomacy. You must understand protocol. Not everyone is skilled in diplomacy. Some people are simply unrefined and unrefinable!

Your dressing may have to be modified if you are to appear in public. Your speech will have to be appropriate and polished for the occasion. Some people simply do not have the background that enables them to function in this role.

Some people are unable to communicate with the public without offending people. Some simply do not have the patience or the ability to be a public relations person. A person who knows how to serve in the public eye is therefore valuable.

9. Having a specialized ability increases your value.

When you have some unusual talent, you become valuable. For instance, your ability to speak an unusual language can increase your value greatly. You must find a place where your particular ability is valued. There are people whose ability to sing has earned them special jobs in special places.

Not everyone has the ability to be a world-class singer. Some people have the ability to type with speed and accuracy. Such things give unusual value to a person. When I began to write books, I discovered how few people really know how to type with speed and accuracy.

The ability to host people and cater for them is also a special skill. Not every woman cares for people in a way that makes them feel at home. Some women actually drive people away with their unfriendly and expressionless faces. Some people do not even bother to learn what to do to make a particular person comfortable. Such motherly hosts are specially endowed and are of great value to churches that host guests frequently.

The ability to be a good public speaker or presenter is a special skill that can increase your value. Such a person may be invaluable for public relations and improving the corporate image of the organization.

Special computer skills and technical abilities can also make a person valuable. Discover what special ability you have and exploit it to the fullest. Let your gift make room for you and take you to the highest place!

10. You are valuable when you save the organization money.

There are people who have the ability to help save money. They negotiate on behalf of the organization as though they were negotiating for their own lives. Such people save lots of money for the ministry through their bargaining skills. People who make purchases and payments for the ministry are often not concerned about how much everything costs. But there are some who care and try to get the best deal every time. Such people are priceless treasures to an organization!

Other people view the opportunity to make a purchase on behalf of the organization as a chance to make some money for themselves. These are dangerous people who slowly undermine the ministry.

Paul said,

For I have no man likeminded, who will naturally care for your state.

Philippians 2:20

11. Your value greatly increases when you can work without supervision.

Supervising people can be one of the most tiresome jobs. Having to constantly monitor what someone is doing is wearisome, to say the least. What a joy it is to have someone who can work with little or no supervision. Just give him the job and he will come back with the results. When you have to chase a person, giving a hundred reminders and promptings about the same thing, you may just want to do the job yourself!

Unfortunately, most people need supervision and cannot be trusted to work on their own. Become someone who works without supervision!

12. Loyalty makes a person valuable.

Loyalty is more important than any qualification or skill I know. Any leader who does not value loyalty will live to discover the pain of treachery. A loyal person is far more valuable than an educated but disloyal person. When an employer does not know the value of loyalty, he often chooses people who are impressive but intrinsically disloyal.

After a while, these impressive people turn out to be painful choices. I have watched as ministers set aside faithful people and choose exciting people who have no loyalty. These people have not learnt about the great value of loyalty.

With the passage of time, most people will prefer a loyal person to any other. Every worker has to choose between his loyalty to the boss and his loyalty to the rest of the workers.

I once told a new employee, "You will either be liked by me or by the people. It's your choice." His value to me would rise greatly if he was loyal to me rather than to the rest of the staff.

13. Good organizers and managers are valuable.

Some people are able to gather people around and make them do their jobs. Others are simply unable to control anyone. I once found out that one of my newly appointed managers was unable to control the janitor. I realized that I had chosen the wrong person to be a manager.

Someone who is incapable of controlling drivers, cleaners and housemaids will not be able to control more educated and confident people. Your value goes up when you are able to control difficult people.

14. You are valuable when you are a contented person.

Satisfied people are a joy to have around.

Better is an handful with quietness...
Ecclesiastes 4:6

Moses had the difficulty of leading a discontented and grumbling crowd. Such people cannot be satisfied by anything. Good relationships are not built on money. No amount of money can make a person happy. Discontented people want more and more but they are never satisfied!

A worker who is happy with the little you can give is truly a valuable person. One discontented person can poison the entire workforce. Such people love to be part of unions, strikes and disruptions of work.

Such things are not needed in the church! Get rid of discontented people. Send them off to get a better job where they will be happier. It is not worth having them around.

15. Your value increases when you can learn anything required.

You may be required to produce television programs. If you are rigid and unprepared to learn completely new things, you will be limited in your value.

People who are prepared to learn new things are valuable! You may be required to run an orphanage or a radio station. Are you prepared to learn a completely new skill? I have watched as lawyers have learnt the art of construction and doctors have learnt how to run bookshops and schools. Their value increased because they were prepared to acquire new skills.

16. Long-standing workers are valuable.

Time speaks! Someone who has been around for years has a value that "Johnny-just-come" does not have! Years of stability and faithful service definitely confer value on every employee. Time tells whether a person is faithful or not!

Time tells whether a person is a liar or not. Time tells whether a person is a thief or not. Time tells whether a person is morally upright or not. The long years spent together assure us that we can depend on you.

17. Spirituality makes you valuable.

Spiritual people are valuable. Every church should endeavour to employ spiritual people. Sometimes spiritual people do not have certain qualities or abilities but their spirituality gives them great value in the ministry setting.

Unfortunately, some churches end up employing all sorts of unspiritual people; even unbelievers. They do this in order to fill some vacancies.

But it is often better not to have anyone, than to have a carnal person working in the church. Someone who has not been spiritual is not likely to become spiritual when he is in full-time ministry.

Gradually, a little leaven leavens the whole lump. Unspiritual and unsaved people gradually dilute the intensity of the zeal and anointing of any ministry. Soon you may have a full-time ministry staff of pseudo-Christians.

Wrong decisions will soon be taken because of the influence of carnal people. Full-time ministry is a place for zealous people who are on fire for Jesus. The Lord said to the Laodecian church, "I wish you were hot." God wants us to be hot and not lukewarm. Lukewarmness is a deadly enemy that destroys every true church.

18. Anointed people are valuable.

An anointed person is a special person with the grace of God operating in his life. Such people have great value because the grace and wisdom of God makes them operate above human ability. It is a joy to watch anointed people as they operate in the gift of God. They are special, they are different and they are wise!

The Spirit of the LORD will rest on Him, the spirit of wisdom and understanding, the spirit of counsel and strength, the spirit of knowledge and the fear of the LORD.
And He will delight in the fear of the LORD, and He will not judge by what His eyes see, Nor make a decision by what His ears hear;

Isaiah 11:2-3, NASB

This is the wisdom that comes through the anointing. May you be an anointed worker!

19. Experienced people are valuable.

Experienced people have an uncanny knowledge of the future. Most things actually work out the way experienced people envisage.

Many things do not happen the way you would expect. There is some special knowledge that comes only through experience. People with experience often turn the tide in a battle. A person's value increases greatly because he is experienced. Do not shy away from things that make you experienced. The more experience you have, the more valuable you become.

20. Morality makes you valuable.

Moral and upright people are especially valuable as you can count on them to do the right thing behind closed doors. Joseph had the opportunity to sleep with his boss' wife but he did not. He could be trusted in very tempting circumstances. Such people are truly valuable.

The presence of one lecherous person (someone who is unduly interested in sex) can spoil the work of many years and end the employment of everyone else.

The higher you go in ministry the deeper your safety pegs must be. When you get to the eighth floor and you lean on the balcony, you would not want to discover that it is made of cardboard! The higher you go, the more the need for stronger character.

21. Working with excellence increases your value.

Sloppy workers who deliver shoddy work are a pain to most employers. They need extra supervision and are stressful to have around. What a joy it is to have someone who delivers a quality job every time! Such people are valuable and it is worth paying the price to have their services.

22. Your choleric personality makes you valuable.

Your choleric personality will make you valuable in difficult projects that need a driving force. This is the personality that will make you valuable in building up something from scratch. Choleric people are usually the best leaders but not very good assistants.

23. Your phlegmatic personality makes you valuable.

If God made you a phlegmatic, you will have special abilities, which no one else has. Phlegmatic people are stable workers and able to carry out monotonous jobs. There are many important jobs, which must go on in spite of their repetitiveness.

Where would we be without teachers and lecturers who stick to their jobs for years? These precious and steady trainers produce the high achievers and skilled workers of tomorrow. Phlegmatic workers are usually valuable because they are good assistants.

24. Your melancholic personality makes you valuable.

Melancholic people are usually very gifted and very organized. They are usually thoughtful, contented and deeply sacrificial. Melancholic people became the great missionaries of the past. These people are often quiet and can work where privacy and secrecy is required.

If God has made you a melancholic, you will be useful for many things in the office environment. You will keep things organized and private. You will have the ability to bring order and good management into places which are often disorganized.

25. Your sanguine personality makes you valuable.

If you are a sanguine, you will not be useful for things which require much organization. The scatter-brained and disorganized sanguine is of no use with sensitive documents. However, without a sanguine, your office will be a sad place! It will be lifeless because the life and excitement of the team is often created by the valuable sanguine. This is where a sanguine is most helpful.

If you put a melancholic in an office which a sanguine should occupy, people will leave because of the silent, stern and unfriendly melancholic.

I value the sanguine people in my office. They have no replacement. All the melancholics and cholerics put together cannot make the contribution of one sanguine.

Chapter 9

How to Enjoy Your Work

It is important to enjoy your work since that is what you will spend most of your time doing - working. Most people do not enjoy work and look forward to the slightest chance to escape.

It is therefore one of the greatest blessings to be given the kind of work that makes use of your God-given qualities.

Work then becomes like play, leisure and pleasure! No longer will you spend your working days longing for a vacation. No longer will you spend your working hours glancing at the clock and wondering why closing time is so far away.

It takes the God-kind of wisdom to enjoy work. You need to apply heavenly wisdom to what you are doing, otherwise you will end up depressed and wondering what life is about.

Even king Solomon, the richest and wisest man that ever lived, found life to be a vexation of spirit. He condemned his working experience on the earth and called it vanity. He spoke of the toil he had undertaken and the uselessness of it all. He considered the future and wondered what would happen to all the things he had built.

He thought to himself, "What if the person who comes after me destroys everything?"

Yea, I hated all my labour which I had taken under the sun: because I should leave it unto the man that shall be after me. And who knoweth whether he shall be a wise man or a fool? yet shall he have rule over all my labour wherein I have laboured, and wherein I have shewed myself wise under the sun. This is also vanity.

Ecclesiastes 2:18-19

As his melancholic thoughts deepened, he could only utter the words, "Vanity of vanities. All is vanity." Indeed, the one who succeeded him was a fool.

The son of the wisest man who ever lived (Rehoboam), indeed demonstrated great folly at his very first cabinet meeting. His very first decision split the kingdom up. The son of the wise man was now left with one tribe out of twelve to govern.

What a drastic reduction of the kingdom that his father had ruled! To make matters worse, he was unable to keep all the gold vessels that King Solomon had heaped up in the temple. Rehoboam replaced the golden vessels with brass - a poor substitute indeed! Solomon's son was a pale reflection of his father.

Such is the futility of all our life's work. It is vanity. Perhaps most working people have not reflected on these realities. If they do they would not find much meaning in what they are doing. This is the difference between secular work and full-time ministry.

When a Christian works for the Lord in full-time ministry, it is still important to apply a certain kind of wisdom.

This wisdom will make you enjoy your work and live joyfully under the sun. The term "under the sun" is used frequently in the book of Ecclesiastes. This phrase speaks of the life we live "under the sun" or the life we live on this earth. Solomon gave us words of wisdom that can dramatically improve life "under the sun".

However, most of the wisdom for life "under the sun" does not give guidance for the life hereafter.

If you fail to apply this wisdom "under the sun" you will probably hate your life in the end. You will find life and work a futile experience. Why would the Queen of Scotland say as she died, "Shame on life"? She sounded just like Solomon.

Therefore I hated life; because the work that is wrought under the sun is grievous unto me: for all is vanity and vexation of spirit.

Ecclesiastes 2:17

Wisdom for Enjoying Your Work

1. Enjoy your work by eating and drinking while you work.

The phrase "eat and drink" refers to having your basic needs met as you work. Eating good food and living well is wisdom that will make you enjoy working.

Some people save up for a good retirement but never reach that age.

Then I commended mirth, because a man hath no better thing under the sun, than to eat, and to drink, and to be merry: for that shall abide with him of his labour the days of his life, which God giveth him under the sun.

Ecclesiastes 8:15

It is time to enjoy your food and drink. Eat what you actually enjoy and drink to your fill. Bring out the best plates in the house and use the nicest glasses. Don't save them up for visitors any more. You are as good as any visitor!

Behold that which I have seen: it is good and comely for one to eat and to drink, and to enjoy the good of all his labour that he taketh under the sun all the days of his life, which God giveth him: for it is his portion.

Ecclesiastes 5:18

2. Be happy and joyful at work.

It is important to be joyful and happy whilst working. You will spend most of your lifetime working. You must enjoy the company of those you work with. You must be able to laugh, holler, and have a good time. If you do this, you will love going to work.

You will actually miss being at work because you will miss the good company and the good fun of it all. Home may even seem boring to you when you are joyful at work.

> **Then I commended mirth, because a man hath no better thing under the sun, than to eat, and to drink, and to be merry: for that shall abide with him of his labour the days of his life, which God giveth him under the sun.**
>
> **Ecclesiastes 8:15**

Fight till you work in the right environment and with the right people.

3. Accept your lot.

> **Then I realised that it is good and proper for a man to eat and drink, and to find satisfaction in his toilsome labour under the sun during the few days of life God has given him-- for THIS IS HIS LOT.**
>
> **Moreover, when God gives any man wealth and possessions, and enables him to enjoy them, TO ACCEPT HIS LOT and be happy in his work-- this is a gift of God.**
>
> **Ecclesiastes 5:18-19, NIV**

Accept what God has given you. God has not given you everything. There are things we all wish we had but everyone must accept his lot. If you do not have a husband and spend all your life fighting to get one, you will probably become bitter and frustrated. If you do not have a child and spend the better part of your adult life trying to have one, you are likely to experience many disappointments.

As long as you do not accept your lot, you will have a life of unwinnable battles and humiliating defeats. "Accept your lot" is the wisdom of God for a happy life under the sun.

4. Enjoy work by living joyfully with your spouse.

> **LIVE JOYFULLY WITH THE WIFE whom thou lovest all the days of the life of thy vanity, which he hath**

given thee under the sun, all the days of thy vanity: FOR THAT IS THY PORTION IN THIS LIFE, and in thy labour which thou takest under the sun.

Ecclesiastes 9:9

One of the ways to enjoy your work is to live happily with your spouse. Anyone who has been married knows that marital conflict is a painful and discomfitting experience. It discolours everything and releases shadows of depression into your entire life. Indeed marital harmony is one of the rewards and blessings a person could have.

Many millionaires live alone and estranged from their wives. Their homes are filled with empty rooms and unused swimming pools. There are no shouts of joy and no peals of laughter from these homes.

Do these millionaires really have the blessings of life "under the sun"? Life is more than a pay package. There are many other things that God teaches us to consider.

It is time for you and your spouse to laugh at each other and enjoy a few moments "under the sun" together.

Do not be fixated on the negatives. There are many things to talk about. Have dinner together! Make tea for each other. Have fun! Enjoy and accept each other's friendship! Do not accuse each other! Play with each other and make light of all the ugliness in your spouse. This world is not our home. We are just passing through and under the sun for a season! Pass your tests of this life under the sun!

5. Eat of your wealth and take your portion as you work.

There is an evil which I have seen under the sun, and it is common among men: A man to whom God hath given riches, wealth, and honour, so that he wanteth nothing for his soul of all that he desireth, yet God giveth him not power to eat thereof, but a stranger eateth it: this is vanity, and it is an evil disease.

Ecclesiastes 6:1-2

Spend money on yourself. Use some of the wealth you have earned on yourself. That is part of enjoying your working life. Invest in your surroundings. If you spend most of your time in your bedroom, make it the nicest bedroom in the world. Have fun with the goodies God has given you. It is an evil thing to be unable to use the wealth you have earned. Failure to eat your portion will make you hate life and hate work.

And I gave my heart to know wisdom, and to know madness and folly: I perceived that this also is vexation of spirit. For in much wisdom is much grief: and he that increaseth knowledge increaseth sorrow.

Ecclesiastes 1:17-18

6. **Remember that people are envious of hard-working people.**

Again, I considered all travail, and every right work, that for this a man is envied of his neighbour. This is also vanity and vexation of spirit.

Ecclesiastes 4:4

This world has six billion selfish, greedy and lazy people. When a hard-working person comes along, he tills the ground, prospers and creates wealth. Unfortunately, his wealth and success only stir up the jealousy of his brothers.

Abel did not do anything to hurt his brother Cain. Cain was jealous of Abel's success and eventually killed him.

Under the sun, hard-working and successful people will always be surrounded by envious people. Successful men all over the world live under the teeming threat of envious people.

Jesus Christ was crucified because of envy. "For he knew that the chief priests had delivered him for envy" (Mark 15:10).

7. **Be content as you work for God.**

Better is an handful with quietness, than both the hands full with travail and vexation of spirit.

Ecclesiastes 4:6

This may be one of the most important strengths that you will ever develop. The ability to be content is so important for full-time ministers and their families. It is this ability that keeps your mind and heart on eternity.

In this all-important spiritual state, you will be content with food, clothes and somewhere to live. This truly is the biblical prescription for all spiritual pilgrims.

8. Patience will make you go further.

Better is the end of a thing than the beginning thereof: and the patient in spirit is better than the proud in spirit.

Ecclesiastes 7:8

Impatience is the brother of discontentment. Impatient people cannot wait for the seeds they have sown to germinate. They must have all the money now. They must have cars, houses, gold and other rewards now and in this life. It is this spirit of impatience that cuts us off many a minister from realizing their full potential.

9. Wisdom will make you work better.

This wisdom have I seen also under the sun, and it seemed great unto me:

Ecclesiastes 9:13

Every job can be made easier and faster through wisdom. Farming, carpentry, fishing and even the practice of medicine are much easier today because wisdom has made everything a little easier. Use wisdom to make whatever work you do faster and more fruitful.

10.Working in twos is always more fruitful and enjoyable.

Two are better than one; because they have a good reward for their labour.

Ecclesiastes 4:9

An eternal law of fruitful work is the law of working in teams of twos. I have tried sending out people alone and I have discovered that two are always better than one. Believe and practise the principle of "two are better than one". It will make your life's work much easier.

Chapter 10

How to Find Your Life's Work

Your life's work is a gift from God. Many people would be surprised to find out that work is actually a gift from God. Without the gift of work, many would be listless, lacking the energy and vitality of life.

It is the work God has given us to do that energizes us. As soon as you sense that the work you are doing is worthless, it is difficult to continue working. This revelation of how futile secular work is, is what spurs many into full-time ministry.

It is difficult to spend all your energy doing something that you know is a waste of time.

Seven Things You Must Know about Work

1. Know that work is better than rest, because God worked six days and rested one day **(Exodus 20:11).**
2. Understand why too much rest is a negative thing. **(Proverbs 6:10-11)**
3. Know that happiness at work is one of the gifts of God. **(Ecclesiastes 5:19)**
4. Know the things that take away the joy of work. **(Songs 2:15)**
5. It is possible to work without craving for leave. **(John 9:4)**
6. Keep searching till you find your life's work. **(Esther 4:14)**
7. Decide to work rather than to play or to rest. **(Nehemiah 4:6)**

Eight Ways to Identify Your Life's Work

1. Your life's work will give a new meaning to your life.

When you find your life's work, it will give you something more than money. There is more to life than the amount of money you have. King Solomon had all the money in the world yet he said, "Vanity of vanities; all is vanity."

2. Your life's work is something God has called you to.

Jesus saith unto them, My meat is to do the will of him that sent me, and to finish his work.

John 4:34

When I followed the call of God on my life, I found my life's work. Many people live and die without beginning their life's work.

3. Your life's work is something that you will not hate.

Solomon hated his work and his life. This is the futility of those whose work is related only to life on this earth. Solomon was depressed and miserable at the end of his life.

Therefore I hated life; because the work that is wrought under the sun is grievous unto me: for all is vanity and vexation of spirit.

Yea I hated all my labour which I had taken under the sun: because I should leave it unto the man that shall be after me.

Ecclesiastes 2:17-18

Solomon's wisdom was the wisdom *under the sun* - the wisdom for life on this earth. As far as earthly achievements were concerned, Solomon accomplished very much. But as he approached the gates of eternity, his earthly accomplishments paled into insignificance. Work that focuses on eternity will not leave you depressed.

Queen Margaret of Scotland at the end of her life said, "Shame on life!"

However, the missionary, dying on his ship in the midst of the sea said, "I go with the gladness of a boy bounding from school. I feel so strong in Christ."

Since I entered into full-time ministry, I have not hated my work or my life. When I worked in the secular world, I hated work and I found my life useless. A little analysis of those ahead of me showed me the futility of all my labour. O what a blessing it is for me to have found my life's work!

4. In your life's work, you will enjoy the rewards of your labour.

Many people do not enjoy the fruits of their hard work. They work all day and all night but never sit down to enjoy the simple benefits of life.

...every man should eat and drink, and enjoy the good of all his labour, it is the gift of God.

Ecclesiastes 3:13

The gift of God enables you to be happy, enjoy the little pleasures, and rest from your labours. When you find your life's work you will experience all these.

5. In your life's work, money will no longer drive you.

When you find your life's work, money will not matter so much anymore. You will work for the joy of fulfilling God's will.

Like Jesus, you will say, "My meat (satisfaction) is to do the will of Him that sent me."

You will also know that a man's life does not consist in the abundance of things that he possesses (Luke 12:15). You will know that money is elusive and no one ever has enough.

He that loveth silver shall not be satisfied with silver; nor he that loveth abundance with increase: this is also vanity.

Ecclesiastes 5:10

6. In your life's work you will not labour in vain.

Working in the world is vanity. Solomon told us that repeatedly. It is working in the Lord that is not vanity. Paul described his

73

work differently. Solomon called his work vanity but Paul said his work was not in vain.

> **Therefore, my beloved brethren, be ye stedfast, unmoveable, always abounding in the work of the Lord, forasmuch as ye know that your labour is not in vain in the Lord.**
>
> **1 Corinthians 15:58**

7. Your life's work makes you become a blessing to others.

As you fulfil God's calling, you will become a blessing to others. God will bless you abundantly and you will help many people.

> **I have shewed you all things, how that so labouring ye ought to support the weak, and to remember the words of the Lord Jesus, how he said, It is more blessed to give than to receive.**
>
> **Acts 20:35**

8. In your life's work your talents will be revealed.

When I worked in the secular world, most of the gifts God had given me were submerged. I was never a leader, I was never appointed to any special position and I did not shine.

In full-time ministry, my abilities and talents have been utilized to the full. I have found a job that taxes my mind and my strength to the uttermost. Working in full-time ministry makes my sleep enjoyable.

> **The sleep of a labouring man is sweet, whether he eat little or much: but the abundance of the rich will not suffer him to sleep.**
>
> **Ecclesiastes 5:12**

Chapter 11

Why Some People Do Not Prosper at Work

Some people do not prosper because they are in the wrong job. Even when you are diligent and hardworking, being in a job you are not suited for will destroy you. You will not shine and you will not excel because you are not born for the kind of job you have chosen.

1. You cannot prosper without a calling.

When you are not called to something, you get into all sorts of difficulties. A train is not designed to fly. No matter how it is positioned on the runway, flying is impossible! It was designed to stay on the ground and to move along rail tracks.

It is important that you find your calling because you are designed to do specific things. Many difficulties come from doing jobs that you are not suited for. Functioning in a call which is not your own is like taking an honour which is not yours.

And no man taketh this honour unto himself, but he that is called of God...

Hebrews 5:4

2. You cannot prosper with the wrong temperament.

Perhaps this is one of the most important points in this book. In a previous chapter we discussed how each temperament is suited for certain jobs. Make sure that you are doing a job suited to your particular temperament. If you are a choleric person, find a leadership job that is suitable for choleric people. If you are phlegmatic, ask to be excused from jobs that require a driving, leadership personality!

It is in your interest that you work according to your particular temperament. If you do not, you will repeatedly be regarded as a failure.

3. You cannot prosper in the wrong company.

If you do not have to sit with sinners all day long, you are truly blessed. Pray that God will give you people whose company you enjoy.

Blessed is the man that walketh not in the counsel of the ungodly, nor standeth in the way of sinners, nor sitteth in the seat of the scornful.

Psalms 1:1

4. You cannot prosper in a meaningless job.

Then I looked on all the works that my hands had wrought, and on the labour that I had laboured to do: and, behold, all was vanity and vexation of spirit, and there was no profit under the sun.

Ecclesiastes 2:11

It is unfortunate to have to do a meaningless job. During the Second World War, one of the punishments given to intelligent professors and scientists was the carrying of rocks from one end of a prison yard to the other.

From morning until evening, they carried these rocks to and fro, creating a heap and then taking it apart when it reached a certain height. It was indeed a sore vexation to these honourable men. Some of them went crazy as they did years and years of this meaningless work. Perhaps that is why you are going crazy at your current job.

5. You cannot prosper working for someone you dislike.

Surely oppression maketh a wise man mad; and a gift destroyeth the heart.

Ecclesiastes 7:7

It is a painful experience to work for someone you dislike. It is truly a joy to work for someone whose company and leadership you enjoy. I pray that you will find an opportunity to work for someone who does not oppress you.

6. You cannot prosper without a proper preparation.

Prepare thy work without, and make it fit for thyself in the field; and afterwards build thine house.

Proverbs 24:27

The lack of preparation makes work a very difficult thing. Preparation is necessary for every job. Sometimes you have not read your notes or prepared adequately. A lack of preparation makes you incapable of your tasks.

This lack of preparation makes work a difficult experience everyday. It is important to prepare yourself adequately so that you will find yourself enjoying the work God has given you.

Chapter 12

How to Have Favour with Your Boss

1. **See him as one who is placed there by God.**

   ...For there is no authority except from God, and those which exist are established by God.

   Romans 13:1

2. **Recognize and relate to him as you would relate with God Himself.**

   Do your work as though you are doing it for the Lord.

   ...with good will doing service, as to the Lord, and not to men:

   Ephesians 6:7

3. **Be humble towards your boss.**

   Humility is the only way to promotion in God's house.

   And whosoever will be chief among you, let him be your servant:

   Matthew 20:27

4. **Learn all you can about your job.**

   A wise man will hear, and will increase learning; and a man of understanding shall attain unto wise counsels

   Proverbs 1:5

   There is a lot to learn every day. We will never stop learning until we die. Open your heart and discover all there is to know about your job.

5. **Listen to instructions carefully.**

   Recognize that the person in authority over you knows something that you don't. That is why he is in that position.

Hear, ye children, the instruction of a father, and attend to know understanding.

Proverbs 4:1

6. Understand the spirit of the instruction.

Long-winded meetings and lengthy discussions are intended to make you understand your instructions. When you understand the spirit of the instruction, you are able to carry out your orders better.

7. Discover what your boss likes and wants, then do it!

There are certain things that please every important person. They often do not care about many things. Often they look out for just one thing and if you can get that right, you will always be in their good books.

Surprisingly, people do a hundred different things that have not been asked for and leave out the one thing that means everything to the boss.

8. Learn what displeases your boss and avoid those things like the plague.

Notice what angers your boss and learn to avoid them. Understand why he is upset by certain things and discover what to do to avoid them. Like I said, it takes very little to please important people. They do not have time for many things. There are just a few things they notice.

9. Learn to anticipate your boss's next move.

How refreshing it is to have a servant who knows what you will do next. It is like a cool drink on a very hot and sunny day. Anticipating your boss's next move is to think the way he thinks and to plan with him in mind. This ability to anticipate things shows a good level of intelligence and is also a sign of partnership.

10. Repeat his instructions to be sure you understand them.

When you receive instructions, develop a habit of repeating what you have heard to make sure you got it right. Sometimes, a slight variation in understanding the instruction can lead to a disaster.

11. Start writing when your boss starts speaking.

This shows you are smart, intelligent and ready for action. Always have a book ready when he calls. There may be nothing to write, but you must be ready. It is discouraging to give a lot of instructions only to find that nothing has been written by a scatter-brained employee.

12. Do not be jumbled up and confused in his presence.

It is important to be composed and ready for every task. Have your note book and pen at hand at all times so that you do not look silly and disorganized.

13. Be dressed properly and decently whenever he is present.

Throw away clothes that are unacceptable and inappropriate so that even in your most casual moments you will be professional and ready for action.

14. Do what you are asked to do immediately.

There is no better time to start carrying out an instruction than right now. Start immediately! Carry out new instructions first and do routine things later. Your boss's heart will warm up to you when you deal with his urgent requests.

15. Never stop routine jobs until instructed.

Some routine activities will never be checked unless there is some problem or other. Often, it is in a time of crisis that the negligence of routine work is discovered. This is the point at which many people lose their jobs.

16. Carry out all instructions to their logical conclusion.

Every boss wants to hear that the mission is accomplished. No supervisor wants to be told about unsolved problems.

He wants to hear about solutions. He wants to hear how you overcame the obstacles you met. Within one command lies a host of challenges that must be overcome. Every boss is looking for problem solvers. Everyone can narrate a string of unsolved problems but who can solve them?

Solve any problems that come up in the course of doing your job. Just make sure you bring your instructions to a thorough conclusion.

17. Become your boss's no.1 problem solver.

Every boss is attracted to solution-bringers, bridge-builders, problem solvers and accomplishers. Never leave unsolved a problem that you could have solved. The one thing that will devalue you in your boss' eyes is when you do not solve problems. Most bosses know that there are a host of problems to be overcome. That is the very reason why he gave you the job.

18. Never criticize your boss publicly or privately.

It will erode your spiritual relationship with him and open the door for demons. Ask the Israelites what happened to them when they began complaining about Moses. A grumbling employee is a liability and I would advise any leader to dismiss all the grumblers.

19. At all costs, avoid the job of the "office complainer".

There are always people who are not happy about something. They have a chronic spirit of murmuring. Make sure you never become the "office complainer".

20. Never be angry or irritated at new instructions.

Do not be upset when instructions are changed. Do not be angry when instructions are repeated. Your job is to be humble and do what you are told. If you get irritated at a change of instructions, you are probably too big for your job.

21. Humbly receive all corrections no matter how long you have been around.

The longer you stay in a job, the more likely you are to think that you know everything. Humble yourself and receive correction. You may have been around for ten years but there are still things to learn.

22. Be spiritual, be restful and be wise.

When you do not use your time wisely, you never have time to pray. It is important to be prayerful and restful. It makes you wiser and more effective. When you are not restful, you become incomplete, inconclusive and untidy. Watch out! Redeem the time because the days are evil.

Redeeming the time, because the days are evil.

Ephesians 5:16

Spiritual leaders always know those around them who are not spiritual.

Chapter 13

How to Choose between Part-Time and Full-Time Ministry

Failure or success in the ministry often hinges on whether to be a full-time minister or to be a lay person. There are many people who should be unpaid church workers but are full-time ministers. There are also part-time ministers who should be in full-time ministry.

When someone called into part-time ministry goes into full-time ministry, he becomes a misfit. He lacks the grace for what he is doing and often misrepresents true ministry. Unfortunately, the church is replete with examples of these errors.

Does the ministry really have to be done on a full-time basis? If it is to be done on a full-time basis, what are the reasons for such a decision? Who should be a full-time minister and who should be a part-time (lay) minister? These are some of the questions this book seeks to address.

Three Ducks in a Vision

Years ago, I was an executive member of a Christian fellowship. Seven people formed the leadership committee.

One day, I had a vision in which I saw three waddling ducks wearing top hats. It was indeed a strange sight. You must know that a top hat is much bigger than the head of a duck.

Obviously, these three ducks were a strange sight to behold. Something was wrong, and something was in the wrong place. Ducks are not supposed to wear hats! Somebody was wearing something he was not supposed to wear.

Somebody in the executive was holding a position he was not supposed to hold. That is what God showed me through this vision.

I began to find out more and to seek God's will concerning this vision. After a while, we discovered that one member of the executive was completely out of place. He did not qualify in the least for the position he held. I do not know how he came to be among us.

By the time we had finished delving into this fellow's issues we had no choice but to ask him to leave the group. It was a painful and embarrassing experience for us all.

I do not wish to go into details, but believe me, the description of a duck wearing a top hat should be enough to explain how inappropriate it was for him to be in the executive.

That is how it is when people are wrongly placed. It is time to move into what God has called you to. You will be rewarded for faithfulness.

If God has called you to full-time ministry, you will be rewarded for doing it faithfully. If He has called you to be a layperson, remain in lay ministry and be faithful.

Are You Called to Full-Time Ministry?

1. If you are not called into full-time ministry, God will not give you the anointing for it.

There will be no oil on your head as you attempt to function in a full-time capacity. It will be just like frying an egg without oil. Let thy head lack no ointment (Ecclesiastes 9:8).

2. If God has not called you into full-time ministry, He will not give you the financial support for it.

Such people often lack the financial support that is necessary. God does not support things that he has not ordained. Because these people do not have God's financial support, they wrongly portray the ministry as a place of great lack.

Such people make ministry look like the most unfortunate vocation a person could ever have. Such people also cause the priesthood to be despised and relegated to school dropouts and people without a future.

3. If you are not called into full-time ministry, God will not protect you in it.

There are many evils in the ministry. Many temptations and trials await full-time ministers. Lay ministry is like walking on the sandy part of the beach but full-time ministry is like walking on rocks.

God is the only one who can protect you in ministry. People do not survive temptations because they are clever! People do not survive attacks of the enemy because they are morally strong! It is the grace of God that carries us through. You will need God's protection. You cannot make it without God's grace.

4. You will make a fool of yourself in full-time ministry if you are not called to it.

You will incur the wrath of God for not staying in your calling. It is important not to force yourself into areas that you have not been called to.

Saul Forced Himself

Saul was a king and not a priest but he forced himself to do priestly work. Samuel told him that he had been a fool.

> **Therefore I said, "Now the Philistines will come down against me at Gilgal, and I have not asked the favor of the LORD.' SO I FORCED MYSELF and offered the burnt offering."**
>
> **Samuel said to Saul, "YOU HAVE ACTED FOOLISHLY; you have not kept the commandment of the LORD your God, which He commanded you, for now the LORD would have established your kingdom over Israel forever."**
>
> **1 Samuel 13:12-13, NASB**

Uzziah Forced Himself

Another example of someone who forced himself into ministry without invitation was Uzziah, the king. The priests warned that "IT APPERTAINETH NOT ONTO THEE". Azariah the priest told Uzziah that it was a sin for him to operate in the office of a priest. He warned, "You will have no honour from the LORD God" (2 Chronicles 26:18).

But when he was strong, his heart was lifted up to his destruction: for he transgressed against the LORD his God, and went into the temple of the LORD to burn incense upon the altar of incense.

And Azariah the priest went in after him, and with him fourscore priests of the LORD, that were valiant men:

And they withstood Uzziah the king, and said unto him, It appertaineth not unto thee, Uzziah, to burn incense unto the LORD, but to the priests the sons of Aaron, that are consecrated to burn incense: go out of the sanctuary; for thou hast trespassed; neither shall it be for thine honour from the LORD God.

Then Uzziah was wroth, and had a censer in his hand to burn incense: and while he was wroth with the priests, the leprosy even rose up in his forehead before the priests in the house of the LORD, from beside the incense altar.

And Azariah the chief priest, and all the priests, looked upon him, and, behold, he was leprous in his forehead, and they thrust him out from thence; yea, himself hasted also to go out, because the LORD had smitten him.

And Uzziah the king was a leper unto the day of his death, and dwelt in a several house, being a leper; for he was cut off from the house of the LORD: and Jotham his son was over the king's house, judging the people of the land.

2 Chronicles 26:16-21

This is a somber warning for those who have not been called into such things. The Bible says that "many" are called but it does not say that "all" are called.

Mistakenly in Lay Ministry

On the other hand, lay people who are supposed to be in full-time ministry are equally out of place. Full-time ministry involves abandoning yourself to God's grace. You can no longer trust in your own strength for your life. You now have to depend on God's supernatural supply of finances. God's call cannot be ignored. You ignore what the Lord has asked you to do at your own peril.

Jesus Was in Full-Time Ministry

Our Lord Jesus was a carpenter. At a point, he laid aside carpentry, and branched into preaching, teaching and healing. What would have happened to us if he had continued to build his carpentry career?

Have this attitude in yourselves which was also in Christ Jesus...

Philippians 2:5, NASB

Peter Was In Full-Time Ministry

Peter was a fisherman. But a time came when he had to stop fishing and follow the Lord. That was full-time ministry. Peter said,

...Behold, we have left everything and followed You.

Mark 10:28, NASB

Paul Was in Full-Time Ministry

Paul was a tent maker. A time came when he gave himself wholly to the Lord and the benefits were seen by all.

More than that, I count all things to be loss in view of the surpassing value of knowing Christ Jesus my Lord, for whom I have suffered the loss of all things, and count them but rubbish so that I may gain Christ.

Philippians 3:8, NASB

Paul explained that he had suffered the loss of everything in order to do the work of God. A lay person does not suffer the loss of all things.

A lay person does not suffer the loss of his job, his profession, his prestige, etc. When you come into full-time ministry you will suffer the loss of many things.

You just have to imagine what it would be like if Peter and Paul had continued in their secular professions. It would truly have been the mother of all sins.

We would not have been saved if Jesus had insisted on being a carpenter. The foundations of the church would not have been laid if Peter had insisted on continuing with his fishing business.

I Despised Full-Time Ministry

When God called me into full-time ministry, I knew that it was of paramount importance that I obey. I had been a very successful lay minister. As a lay minister, I had built a church and had a sizeable congregation. I had won many souls without being in full-time ministry.

I actually prided myself in working for God without being paid. I remember one occasion when I stood by the gate of my house talking to my friend Uncle James. I told him how I had won so many souls that week. I also told him how I did not think there was a need to do the ministry on a full-time basis.

However, at the end of 1990 the Lord directed me differently. He said very clearly, "Give thyself wholly to me and to the ministry." At that time I was a doctor turned businessman but I knew then that the Lord wanted me to go all out in the Ministry.

I love obeying the Lord and I find His commands quite exciting. It was a new challenge for me and an exciting one at that. I began what I call full-time ministry from January 1991. I have been serving the Lord full-time ever since. I have never looked back and I have never regretted that decision. I am blessed to be a full-time minister.

You must seek God in full-time ministry so that all His plans will come to pass.

Chapter 14

Accept The Season of Full-Time Ministry

To every thing there is a season, and a time to every purpose under the heaven:
Ecclesiastes 3:1

God sometimes gives very contrasting instructions. "I know both how to be ABASED, and I know how to ABOUND: every where and in all things I am instructed both to be FULL and to be HUNGRY, both to ABOUND and to SUFFER NEED" (Philippians 4:12) Paul explains that he had received instructions from the Lord. Once he was asked to be full, at another time he was asked to be hungry. Sometimes he was asked to be abased and at other times he was asked to abound.

Dear Christian friend, if you think that God is going to say the same thing all the time, think again. God is not a computer, neither is he a robot. He will lead us when, how and where He wants to.

The Moving Pillar

The children of Israel had to learn to follow the moving pillar of God. There were times the cloud would stay in a place and all the Israelites would camp there. There were times the cloud would move on.

The LORD was going before them in a pillar of cloud by day to lead them on the way, and in a pillar of fire by night to give them light, that they might travel by day and by night.
Exodus 13:21, NASB

Why did it stay sometimes and why did it move on other days? Somebody would have said, "Can't God make up His mind?

Does He want us to stay or go? Are we little children to be tossed to and fro? God! Make up Your mind! Are we travelling by day or by night?"

Questioning God will not help you. Learning to bend, to flow, to yield and to give in will help you in your walk with God.

In my walk with God, I have found that there is no fixed method by which God operates. You simply need to put your ear to Heaven and to receive daily guidance from the Holy Spirit. In your ministry, there may be a season for lay people to do a substantial portion of the pastoral work. However, there may be another season for full-time workers to take up the mantle.

Some years ago, there were hardly any full-time workers in my ministry. Most of the work was done by lay people. The lay people were fantastic champions who built churches in many countries of the world.

But a time came when the Lord began to lead me to increase the number of full-time workers. On one occasion, he asked me to employ twenty more people. I did not know what work these twenty people would do. I resisted the Lord but He repeated the instruction until I obeyed Him. Mysteriously, we needed far more than twenty new employees.

The Cloud Moves

As the years have gone by, the emphasis of my ministry has shifted from lay people to full-time people. Large sections of the outreaches and new missions are run by full-time ministers.

The Lord told me about how He had shifted the mantle from the lay ministry to full-time ministry.

I Called for Full-Time Workers

As led by the Spirit, I began to encourage people to come into full-time ministry. For a season, God gave me messages that centred on coming into full-time ministry.

I preached powerful messages about being set free from working for Pharaoh (a type of Satan and the world system).

I preached about sacrifice and the need to take up the cross.

I taught a series on "proton" in which I encouraged them to choose God first.

I taught on another Greek word "Bebelos" (which means, to despise sacred things) and admonished them not to despise working for God in the ministry.

I taught on the parables of Jesus and how the kingdom was a treasure for which everything must be sacrificed. There was a frantic call for all-out commitment.

Sadly, large sections of the lay fraternity rejected this call. I tried so hard to personally recruit people to join the sacred group of full-time priests. I shared visions and dreams. I read poems to the pastors and the church. I wept over some of them asking what greater honour they wanted from the Lord?

Amazingly, I had very little response from the oldest and most faithful lay pastors. Most of them could not make the transition to full-time ministry.

Enter the Outsiders

In the end, a completely new group of people came from nowhere in response to my frantic calls. They were mostly new and unfamiliar faces. They were young, unknown and untested people.

Many of them were women with little or no pastoral capabilities. Naturally, many of them were not welcomed by the old guard. They steadily filled the places that I thought belonged to my older, faithful lay pastors.

The season had changed, but many could not see what was happening. God was moving on! The same God who had instructed us to do the lay ministry was instructing us to launch into full-time ministry. The God who had anointed me to write a book on lay people and the ministry was leading me to recruit full-time ministers.

The same God who instructed Paul to abase, was now instructing him to abound.

Lamb or Lion

Jesus Christ is both a lamb and a lion. In the book of Revelation, He is called "the Lamb of God that taketh away the sins of the world". However, He is also called "the Lion of the tribe of Judah". Dear friend, a lion is very different from a lamb. Can the same person that appeared as a lion, also appear as a lamb?

It is so important to understand this principle. It is amazing to find these completely contrasting descriptions in the same passage.

And one of the elders said to me, "Stop weeping; behold, THE LION that is from the tribe of Judah, the Root of David, has overcome so as to open the book and its seven seals."

And I saw between the throne (with the four living creatures) and the elders A LAMB standing, as if slain, having seven horns and seven eyes, which are the seven Spirits of God, sent out into all the earth.

Revelation 5:5-6, NASB

If you told people to expect a lamb and then a lion showed up, there would be chaos! The kind of preparations you need to handle the visit of a lion are different from what you need to handle a lamb. Preaching about the lion will sound very different from preaching about a lamb.

When you are used to "lamb sermons" and your pastor comes up with a "lion sermon", you are likely to say he has changed or backslidden. But perhaps you are the one who does not have the heart to flow and yield to the Spirit.

Killing the Messiah

The children of Israel prayed for the Messiah for years and years but when He appeared, they put Him to death. They could not recognize the answer to their own prayer. Jesus walked with the two disciples on the road to Emmaus but they could not recognize Him because He appeared in a different form. Notice the Scripture:

After that HE APPEARED IN ANOTHER FORM unto two of them, as they walked, and went into the country.

Mark 16:12

If Jesus appeared in another form, would you recognize Him? Perhaps you can only recognize Jesus in a particular form. It is time to be flexible and see when God is working in different ways. Perhaps you only recognize the lay ministry. Perhaps you only recognize full-time ministry. It is time to recognize Jesus in whichever form He appears.

Chapter 15

Seven Wrong Perceptions About
Full-Time Ministry

To many outsiders, the concept of being in full-time ministry is absurd. "What is there to do?" they ask. "Can't I come at the weekend to help the church? Do I really have to leave my job? Is it necessary to go to such extremes? We must be cautious! We must be careful! We must not take drastic and emotional decisions!"

1. Wrong perception #1: There is nothing important to do in ministry.

To many lay people, full-time ministry is unnecessary. They do not see why such a move is necessary. This is why I teach about the mysterious purposes of full-time ministry.

I call it mysterious because it is not easy to see what there is to be done in the house of God.

A Lazy Priest?

After all, the church looks like a place where a lazy priest offers sleepy prayers to God all week. At the weekend, this priest will conduct one funeral service, one wedding and one christening. He will then read out his sermon on Sunday and return to his home to continue his long rest!

Why should a doctor, lawyer, or the treasurer of a bank leave their important careers only to work in such a place as a church?

I do not blame anyone who thinks it is not worth it. That is the picture you may have from the outside. The kingdom of Heaven is like a treasure hidden in a field. There are many hidden things about the kingdom of God. Even the work that has to be done is not obvious. The purpose for anyone being in full-time ministry is indeed mysterious.

Jesus said, if you do my will THEN you will know that it is good. Knowing the greatness of the will of God comes by doing it and not just by reading about it. Somehow, it was only after working in full-time ministry that I truly appreciated the work of a priest.

If anyone is willing to do His will, he will know of the teaching, whether it is of God or whether I speak from Myself.

John 7:17, NASB

It is only when you actually enter full-time ministry that you will discover what it is. That is when you will know God's mysterious purpose for full-time ministry.

2. Wrong perception #2: The ministry is not actually work.

When I started full-time ministry, my wife was often asked, "So your husband doesn't work anymore?" There is a perception that ministry is not work.

That is why people want to be counselled on the pastor's day-off. They do not understand that to counsel someone is actually work.

I Will Come in the Afternoon

Some years ago, a lady applied for a job in the ministry. We finally agreed that she should work with us and even gave her a letter of appointment. A few days before she was to start work, she received a job offer from some other organization. To my surprise, she accepted the other job and asked whether she could do the church's work on some afternoons and weekends. I was taken aback.

I realized that this lady did not appreciate the amount of work she would have to do in the ministry. I told her, "I do not think you are ready for full-time ministry."

Somehow, this lady did not even understand why I rejected her proposal to work in the church in the afternoons. I realized that she did not appreciate what full-time ministry was.

3. Wrong perception #3: Full-time ministry is a step downwards.

Moving from secular work into full-time ministry is a step upwards. It is not a step downwards! The Apostle Paul said that he counted all things as dung for the excellency of the knowledge of Christ.

This means that to set aside your medical, legal or engineering profession is the same as flushing away your faeces. No one cries when he flushes away his faeces (unless he is suffering from coprophilia).

To set aside your job as the treasurer of a bank and to take up ministry is like dumping a bag of faeces and taking up a bag of diamonds!

4. Wrong perception #4: Full-time workers have a lot of time on their hands.

That is why full-time workers are sometimes treated as though they are not employed. Relatives and friends of full-time workers love to send them on different errands. Some full-time ministers are made to baby-sit and do house chores by their spouses. These spouses despise ministry and that is why they assign an array of odd jobs to their partners.

5. Wrong perception #5: Ministry can be done after retirement.

Many people would like to work for God but they want to do it after they have accomplished something else. They give their best years to their lofty secular goals and ambitions. They hope that God's work will be waiting for them when they finally retire!

After all God's work can wait! It is not that important. Do you think God can wait for you? I am sorry, God cannot wait for anyone! Souls are dying. Thousands of souls would have died and gone to Hell by the time you finish fulfilling your dreams.

By the time you are older, you will be less active, less energetic, slower, more easily tired, full of the sicknesses of middle age, less able to learn new things, unable to do a full day's work, heavily in debt, and GENERALLY LESS USEFUL TO GOD!

Why do you want to give God an expired and worn out vessel? Give that to the bank!! Give that to the corporate world!! It is time to give your best to God!

It may shock you to know that God has his own retirement package. He also wants young, fresh, able-bodied people to serve in His temple.

GOD DOES NOT WANT THE LEFTOVERS AND REJECTS OF THE WORLD TO BE HIS PRINCIPAL WORKERS.

He defined the age bracket of His workers and asked Moses to retire priests after a certain age. Amazingly, the prime period for doing God's work is between the ages of twenty-five and fifty.

Shockingly, the retirement age for priests is even lower than the world's retirement age.

Then the LORD spoke to Moses, saying, "This is what pertains to the Levites: From twenty-five years old and above one may enter to perform service in the work of the tabernacle of meeting; And at the age of fifty years they must cease performing this work, and shall work no more. They may minister with their brethren in the tabernacle of meeting, to attend to needs, but they themselves shall do no work. Thus you shall do to the Levites regarding their duties.

Numbers 8:23-26, NKJV

Yet another Scripture gives the age of doing God's work as between the ages of thirty and fifty.

Take a census of the descendants of Kohath from among the sons of Levi, by their families, by their fathers' households, FROM THIRTY YEARS AND

**UPWARD, EVEN TO FIFTY YEARS OLD, all who
enter the service to do the work in the tent of meeting.**

Numbers 4:2-3, NASB

God wants the best for His church. The grey-haired men and
women of wisdom have a role in the church. The retirees of this
world also have their place in God's house. But the prime work
of ministry is to be done by able-bodied people between the ages
of twenty-five and fifty. For-… for-… for-… forgive!

6. Wrong perception #6: Ministry does not require educated people.

Many people think that ministry does not require educated or
intelligent people. Ministry is considered a job for dropouts and
a haven for the intellectually less endowed. Why should God's
work have such educated people?

God gave us the dearest and the best. He gave us Jesus Christ.
Jesus was nailed on the tree for you and for me. If the dearest
and the best gave Himself, should we not give our best to Him? I
believe that the dearest and the best kind of people must be given
to the service of God.

7. Wrong perception #7: Full-time ministry makes you an insignificant member of society.

When a person says, "I am the Managing Director of such and
such a company" he sounds important.

When he says, "I am the Treasurer of Barclays Bank" he
sounds very important.

But when he says, "I work in a church" he seems to have lost
his lustre.

Most of the time there is little glamour associated with the
work of the ministry. But in reality, ministry is the most important
job in society.

Where Millionaires Kneel

Someone said to his son who was entering full-time ministry, "You are doing the right thing."

He continued, "It is only in the church that a millionaire can be asked to kneel down and have hands laid on him."

No millionaire will kneel down before his bank manager, he explained. But in the church the millionaire will kneel down before his pastor for prayer.

Chapter 16

Why You Must Choose Full-Time Ministry

He hath shewed thee, O man, what is good; and what doth the LORD require of thee...

Micah 6:8

God will show us what is good and what is required of us. We cannot do His work in our own way. It is His work and it must be done His way, using His methods.

Full-time ministry is God's ordained method of administering His church. No one is wiser than God is.

I believe there was a time I thought I knew better than God on this matter. Mercy! Forgive!

I was a successful lay pastor and had started a church that was growing. I was called Reverend and even had assistant pastors. I was winning souls on a weekly basis through dawn broadcasts, crusades and other programmes.

I prided myself in the fact that I was not a financial burden to the church. Our church was not under any kind of financial pressure and the wisdom of lay ministry was working well.

Did I Know Better than God?

One day, I travelled to Geneva and had a discussion with an American Pastor who had a ministry there. At a point, I told him that I was not paid by my church.

I proudly explained how I supported myself in the ministry. He listened to me and seemed to be impressed.

I told him, "We don't receive tithes and sometimes we don't even take offerings. We do not burden our church financially in any way."

However, at a point, he said, "You are not wiser than God. God has ordained His church to run in a certain way."

He continued, "There is a blessing that comes on a congregation when they pay tithes." He explained how there is a blessing in accepting God's method of running His own church.

Somehow, this conversation stayed with me and I began to study and to seek for God's ordained method of running his church.

Lay Ministry Is Not God's Ordained Way

Even so hath the Lord ORDAINED that they which preach the gospel should live of the gospel.

1 Corinthians 9:14

When something is ordained to be a certain way, it means it is intended, predestined and designed to be that way. God intended and designed that preachers should be paid for preaching the Gospel.

Preaching without being paid is a special arrangement that God allows and blesses at certain times. The Apostle Paul practised this unpaid style of lay ministry better than anyone else. But he is the one who also taught that God's intended method of running the ministry was for pastors to be paid from the work they do.

Lay ministry cleverly removes the burden of looking after priests. It is a wise and helpful method of building a church. I have actually written a book about Lay Ministry. I believe in the lay ministry and have not changed my doctrine. However, God's Word contains many different things, which sometimes look contradictory to the unlearned.

Lay ministry and full-time ministry do not contradict each other. Actually, they complement each other.

The wisdom of lay ministry does not cancel out the need for full-time ministry. Full-time ministry is a ministry of "priests" and "helpers of priests" who work in the temple.

These priests are supported by the offerings and gifts brought to the Lord by the people. The full-time *priests* and *helpers* of priests are to live off the gifts and sacrifices in the temple.

Living off the Gospel

Do ye not know that they which minister about holy things live of the things of the temple? and they which wait at the altar are partakers with the altar?

Even so hath THE LORD ORDAINED THAT THEY WHICH PREACH THE GOSPEL SHOULD LIVE OF THE GOSPEL.

1 Corinthians 9:13-14

God has ordained priests to live off their jobs as preachers. "So also the Lord directed those who proclaim the gospel to get their living from the Gospel" (1 Corinthians 9:14, NASB). This is a very humbling thing for people who could have had other jobs.

It sounds nicer to say, "I earn money from my secular job and I work for God without charge." It sounds very sacrificial indeed!

But it is better to accept God's method of running His church than to do anything else. Don't forget that obedience is better than sacrifice.

Is a Salary from the Church Stolen Money?

Living off a church salary is a little different from living off a salary from the bank. Living a life that depends on offerings and gifts can be even more unsettling.

It seems more acceptable to drive a car you bought whilst working in the bank. Sometimes living in a nice home that was acquired through church money does not seem right. It is almost as though you are using pilfered goods.

But it is important to accept God's ordained method of administering His church and looking after His priests. Are you called of God? Does God want you to be in full-time ministry? Then get ready to live a different kind of life.

Why Preachers Earn Money

1. Every true minister is worthy of his pay.

Do not acquire gold, or silver, or copper for your money belts, or a bag for your journey, or even two tunics, or sandals, or a staff; for the worker is WORTHY of his support.

Matthew 10:9-10, NASB

This verse means that a preacher *ought to have* support. He has *earned* an income. It means he is *justified to receive* money and he truly merits it.

2. Ordained preachers are to live off their jobs as preachers.

God wants His preachers to live in a particular way. He wants to provide for them and pay them Himself for preaching His Word.

3. God has changed the way preachers earn money.

Jesus called His disciples and changed their professions. They lived by fishing. He offered them a new way of making money - winning souls.

As He was going along by the Sea of Galilee, He saw Simon and Andrew, the brother of Simon, casting a net in the sea; for they were fishermen.

And Jesus said to them, "Follow Me, and I will make you become fishers of men..."

Mark 1:16-17, NASB

4. Anyone who refuses God's ordained method is choosing his own way.

Every true minister must desire to walk in what God has prescribed for His priests.

There is a way which seemeth right unto a man, but the end thereof are the ways of death.

Proverbs 14:12

5. Living a life dependent on income from preaching is one of the signs that you are a priest.

The true priests of God lived in this way. Your method of acquiring possessions such as a home, a car, etc, shows where you work.

But I have used none of these things: neither have I written these things, that it should be so done unto me: for it were better for me to die, than that any man should make my glorying void.

1 Corinthians 9:15

Paul declared that though he could have benefited materially from his work as a priest he did not. He did not want anyone to speak evil of his ministry.

6. Preachers deserve the benefits they receive.

And remain in the same house, eating and drinking what they provide, for the laborer deserves his wages...

Luke 10:7, RSV

The eating and the drinking of a true preacher must be at the expense of those preached to. Those are the instructions of our Saviour.

Jesus explains why pastors should eat and drink at the expense of their hosts. He said, "You deserve it."

After ministering, you deserve to be paid. Jesus said preachers deserve salaries!

I deserve to be paid for preaching, teaching, writing, ministering, counselling, encouraging people, talking to people, praying for people, and the list goes on!

Preachers deserve cars, houses, servants and food!

All these are products of wages!

Do not let anyone deceive you with false humility and self-righteousness!

7. Full-time ministers are supposed to collect money from the people.

And those indeed of the sons of Levi who receive the priest's office have commandment in the Law TO COLLECT a tenth from the people, that is, from their brethren, although these are descended from Abraham.

Hebrews 7:5, NASB

The King James Version says priests are COMMANDED TO TAKE TITHES from the people.

Taking and collecting tithes is actually a direct command from God. That means that it is a sin not to collect these tithes. Do not let any worldly person move you away from God's ordained and prescribed method.

8. It is better to obey than to sacrifice your wages.

Samuel replied,

Has the Lord as much pleasure in your burnt offerings and sacrifices as in your obedience? OBEDIENCE IS FAR BETTER THAN SACRIFICE. He is much more interested in your listening to him than in your offering the fat of rams to him.

1 Samuel 15:22, TLB

You will be more pleasing to God if you humbly receive your wages than if you make any unwanted sacrifices. Not all commands of God involve suffering and pain. Do not be wiser than God!

Chapter 17

How God Called Me to
"Give Myself Wholly"

...GIVE THYSELF WHOLLY to them; that thy
profiting may appear to all.

1 Timothy 4:15

...throw yourself into your tasks so that EVERYONE
MAY NOTICE YOUR IMPROVEMENT AND
PROGRESS.

1 Timothy 4:15, TLB

At the end of 1990 the Lord spoke to me. He said, "From now on, I want you to give yourself wholly to my work." I knew what that meant. He explained that if I gave myself completely to the work of God my "profiting" would appear to all. That meant that people would see my progress in ministry.

Armed with this Scripture, I launched into full-time ministry in January of 1991. I have been in full-time ministry, totally dedicated to kingdom business since then. I can say that my little progress and improvement has become evident to some people. The fact that you are reading this book attests to this fact.

Unfortunately, many give themselves half-heartedly to the ministry. That is why they do not make significant strides in it. If you suggested to your boss that you would come to work twice a week in the evenings, do you think he would accept you? Certainly not! The inputs you can make by giving a couple of evenings is different from what you can do when you spend the whole day working. Suggest to your boss that you will work for him only on Sunday afternoons and see if he will keep you. Your value to him would drop sharply.

By this same logic, your value to God is reduced if you are available to Him only on Sunday afternoons. God wants to have people who work for Him during the day and not only in the evenings. Why do you want to be a night officer for Christ?

To give yourself wholly to the Lord means to give everything you are and everything you possess to Jesus. How do you give everything to God? What does it mean to give yourself wholly to the Lord?

1. "Give thyself wholly" means to give your heart.

Many people who work in the secular world have not given their hearts to what they are doing. To give yourself wholly means you must first of all give your heart. Whilst working in the government hospital, I noticed that many of the doctors did not give their hearts to what they were doing. Most of them were looking for an opportunity to leave the country.

Prostitutes give their bodies to their clients but they do not give their hearts. One of the rules of prostitutes is to never kiss a client. Doing something physically does not mean that your heart is in it. Full-time ministry is not something you can do without giving your heart.

This is why full-time ministry is not the same as taking up another secular job. It is the giving of your heart to God. It is the pouring out of your soul into God's work and leaving nothing behind!

People who work in the bank are not pouring out their souls. They are merely looking for more money and higher positions. When you give your heart to the Lord's work, you will see the difference.

2. "Give thyself wholly" means to give your mind, intelligence and ideas.

Full-time ministry involves bringing your intelligence to bear on God's work. Intelligence is not only required in banks, hospitals, science laboratories, political parties, factories, law firms, farms and consultancies. Intelligence is required to do God's work. God's work is not the lowest calling. It is the highest calling! It is the greatest job! Maybe you have despised God's work and given your intelligence and ideas to the building of earthly institutions.

Instead of God's kingdom benefiting from your clever suggestions, it is political parties and banks that do. They make more money and accomplish more of their goals by using your ideas. God could equally use your intelligence and creativity.

I did very well in school. In 1982, there were hundreds of applicants for the only accredited medical school in Ghana. In order of merit, I was the fifth person in the whole country to be interviewed for entry into the medical school.

Whilst in medical school, I earned a distinction and won a prize, which was given to the two best students in the fifth year. God had truly blessed me with intelligence through which I became a medical doctor.

After seven years of medical training and a year of housemanship, God called me to apply the intelligence He had given me to ministry. After all, it was the Lord who had given me everything I had. It was the Lord who had made me excel in school. As the Scripture says,

> **For who maketh thee to differ from another? and what hast thou that thou didst not receive? now if thou didst receive it, why dost thou glory, as if thou hadst not received it?**
>
> **1 Corinthians 4:7**

The kingdom needs intelligent, educated people who can make a difference. To be successful in ministry you will need more than the anointing and miracles. You will need intelligence, good ideas and creativity. I believe that throwing in the numerous good ideas and thinking abilities God has given me has made a difference to the ministry.

God has blessed me with a number of highly educated and intelligent professionals who make a lot of difference to the ministry. Actually, these clever people are gifts given to me by the Lord. They make such a difference to all that happens in our church. They have humbly acknowledged that what they are is just a gift from God.

Indeed, it is a privilege to be called upon to serve the Master with the intellect He has given you.

3. "Give thyself wholly" means to give your education and training.

After being educated and trained by Pharaoh, Moses launched out into God's will and built Israel into a nation. Obviously, he was trained in Pharaoh's palace to rule and to govern nations. Your education and training will be useful to God.

When I entered full-time ministry, people were aghast, saying, "How could you abandon your medical profession and become a pastor?" They said this only because they despised God's work.

Sadly, the kingdom of God is despised and is esteemed to be worthy of only emotionally unstable and uneducated people.

Five Doctors Become Presidents

As I write this book, I know of five medical doctors who have launched campaigns to become the president of Ghana. One of them is an obstetrician/gynaecologist who used to live and work in America. Another is a cardio-thoracic surgeon who used to live and work in Germany. The third one is a pathologist who used to live and work in England. The fourth is practising medicine in the U.S.A. The fifth of these has his own medical practice in one of the cities of Ghana.

It is interesting that these highly trained specialists are not criticized for leaving their field of training to jump into politics. Even though politics is what we know it to be, no one seems to think that it is a waste of their education and training. The ministry is an even higher calling. It is a demanding job, which requires intelligent, well-trained people to give of themselves. Currently, I work with some twelve medical doctors who have set aside medicine for the ministry.

Their training in medicine makes them more capable to do the tasks set before them. I am proud of them and blessed to have such noble people join me in this great calling.

I also have at least eight lawyers who have set aside their law practice to take up ministry.

The list goes on and I could tell you of pharmacists, architects, engineers, IT consultants, bankers and accountants who work full-time in the ministry. They are fully engaged in building God's kingdom by applying their education and training to their new tasks.

4. "Give thyself wholly" means to give your personality and temperament.

God has made us all differently. Some people are choleric, others are melancholic, others sanguine and yet others phlegmatic. A choleric is good at work involving leadership. A melancholic person is good at work involving details and administration. A sanguine is good at work that involves human relations and the phlegmatic is the best at steady and monotonous jobs. All these features are God-given and are important for the progress of any venture.

Businesses, banks and corporations employ people based on these natural abilities. Temperament tests are done routinely by Human Resource Departments.

To give yourself wholly is to take whatever temperament you have and apply it to the church. There are several areas of work, which require your particular temperament. I place people mainly according to their temperaments.

Why do you want to give your God-given temperament to the world? Is it not the greatest opportunity to give something back to God? Do you feel that giving it to the world is more worthwhile? It is time to stop despising the church. Let's give ourselves wholly to the Lord.

God made me choleric and melancholic. When I was in school, I was not seen as anything special. I was never chosen to be a prefect or a leader. But God who created me and put within me my temperament, chose me to be a leader for His people. I could have used my God-given ability to build a bank or a nightclub.

He Built Nightclubs

I recently met a young man who had great leadership abilities. He had built a well-known computer firm and was doing very well. One day, I needed to see him and we set up an appointment in his office.

When we got there, I asked him, "What goes on here? I thought this was your office."

He answered, "Actually, this is a night club as well. Daytime for certain things and night-time for the night club."

"Wow," I said. "I did not know you were into night clubs. Does your wife come here sometimes?"

"Not really, she does not enjoy night life much," he answered.

Some weeks later, I happened to be in another town ministering in one of our churches. When I looked out of the window, I saw a building with a familiar sign and I asked. "What is that building and what do they do there?"

"Oh, it's a night club belonging to so and so."

To my amazement it belonged to the same person. I realized that this man had built a chain of night clubs.

The question is, what will you use your God-given temperaments and abilities for? You can use your gifts to build nightclubs, banks or businesses. I choose to use my abilities to build churches!

Melancholism at Work

God made me melancholic. I often find myself analyzing things and thinking deeply about issues. This ability helped me to analyze loyal and disloyal behaviour, even when it was not obvious.

It has contributed to the things that I have taught over the years. A conversation, which means nothing to someone, becomes a revelation to me because of this analytic gift.

I also find myself arranging and reorganizing what needs to be reorganized. This melancholic nature has helped me to administer and manage churches in different countries of the world.

I have been able to organize many things at the same time because of this "grace" of melancholism. To give yourself wholly is to pour everything you are into God's work until the benefits are seen.

5. "Give thyself wholly" means to give your family.

To give yourself wholly also means to give your family to the Lord. Sadly, there are many ministers who do not want their children to be in the ministry. The Levites served the Lord with their entire families. Their wives and children belonged to the service of God's tabernacle. Give your husband, wife and children to God! Some ministers withhold their wives and use them as a business outreach to make money on the side. They fulfil their secular and business dreams through their wives.

It is important that we examine our hearts and see whether we have given ourselves wholly to God's will. Ask yourself: "If ministry is a good thing, why do I not want my child to be a minister?"

Why do you want him to be a pilot or a lawyer rather than a minister of the Gospel? Do you not believe in your own profession?

6. "Give thyself wholly" means to give your background.

Everybody has a family. We all come from somewhere. This fact was seen even in the life of Jesus. The genealogy of Christ goes to great lengths to describe his origins and heritage. He was the lion of the tribe of Judah and not the lion of the tribe of Benjamin. Christ came from Judah and not from Reuben. Where do you come from? It affects you and your calling!

To give yourself wholly means to allow all that is in your background to help the ministry advance. Your background is one of God's gifts to you. It will enable you to do things that no one else can.

The Half-Caste

I am half-caste. Because of this background, there are certain things I cannot do. In my home, Ghanaian languages were not spoken. English was the language my father spoke to my mother. This limited my ministry's entry into certain areas of the country. It was difficult to establish churches where English was not spoken. It took us years to make a headway in these places.

However, the English-speaking nature of our ministry gave me great access to international fields. I found myself easily establishing churches in other countries. After a while, I realized that my background had played a role in what I could accomplish.

7. "Give thyself wholly" means to give your time.

Many people who work in the secular world do not give themselves wholly to their work. They look forward to the end of the working day and yearn for holidays. When I worked in the hospital, I longed for the end of the day.

I longed to get away from the wards and the clinics. I dreamed of holidays where I would not have to come to this dreary hospital. I counted the available holidays in the year and complained about the brevity of the leave period.

Giving God a daily ten-minute prayer time and a weekly two-hour Sunday morning service is not full-time ministry. Full-time ministry is much more than that. It is to give all of your time to the Lord.

One brother who had worked in a gold mine for years remarked, "I had never worked so hard till I came to work in the ministry. When I worked for the gold mine we would close at five o'clock and I would drop everything and leave. I never thought about the office until I got back the next day."

He continued, "Now, I take work home with me and the work never ends. It's day and night and it goes on and on."

That is how full-time ministry is. All of your time is given to God.

My ministry does not end when I walk out of church. My mind is always on God and His work. There is nothing like a closing time for me. Every moment and everyday belongs to Him now. I do not think of going on leave anymore, neither do I think of retirement.

8. "Give thyself wholly" means to give your money and your assets.

When I began in the ministry, my car was the church bus. My personal stereo became the church's public address system. You have to put everything into the ministry if it is to work. There is a certain throwing in of everything that is necessary for success in ministry. What are you withholding from the Lord?

Looking back at my life, I realize how much I have thrown into the ministry. I threw in office equipment that I owned. I used my father's office as the church's office. I made all my money and everything I owned available for God's work. I believe that all this is part of *giving thyself wholly.*

9. "Give thyself wholly" means to give your energy.

You will experience tiredness in ministry. But I call it sweet exhaustion. You are tired but there is joy bubbling in your heart. It is said that the world is run by tired men. I can assure you that real ministry involves much hard work.

A Foolish Death

One day, a friend of mine visited Sierra Leone. He told me how he found several of the peacekeeping soldiers involved in different businesses. Some of them had become taxi drivers and others were involved in diamond mining. So I asked, "How do soldiers who are supposed to be fighting and keeping the peace become taxi drivers and diamond miners?"

He answered, "They don't want to die a foolish death."

I asked, "What is a foolish death?"

He explained, "They are frustrated with a hopeless war and see no reason why they should die for a worthless cause."

You see, these soldiers sensed the inconsequential nature of the battle they were involved in. They knew that if they were to die they would have sacrificed themselves for nothing.

In the ministry, that feeling of chasing worthless goals goes away. The emptiness that comes with heaping up unusable treasures is gone. There is a great motivation to pour out your energy and your very life for an eternal cause.

10. "Give thyself wholly" means to give your life.

Many people have died on their jobs. Some of them died at work and in the course of duty. Soldiers die at work! Police officers on duty are killed all the time! Numerous doctors are infected with viruses and germs from their patients!

Businessmen and politicians die of stress and heart attacks. Pilots die in plane crashes and the list goes on. All these deaths are related to their jobs.

To give yourself wholly means to work for God even if you lose your life. It means to be ready to die doing His will.

When you give yourself wholly, you will be prepared to be a missionary in dangerous countries. There are many things in the ministry that will expose you to danger but in full-time ministry you can give yourself wholly to dangerous things.

The Airline Steward

Some time ago, I offered a job to an airline steward. He accepted the ministry opportunity but said he would have to speak to his father. His father was not happy that his son would work in a church and indicated that he would like to talk with me about it.

This man wanted to talk me out of his son's employment. But I refused to speak to the young man's father.

I made it clear that I would be prepared to speak to the father if it was about salvation, the Holy Spirit or any spiritual problem.

But if the discussion was about his son's employment then I would not to speak to him. My reasoning was simple.

When this steward applied to work for the airline his father did not ask to see the Managing Director of the airline.

Apart from being almost bankrupt, this airline was known to be dangerous and poorly maintained.

Was it not more dangerous for his son to work for this airline than for him to work in the church? Why did this father want to speak to me to prevent his son from working for the Lord? People simply have no respect for the church!

People risk their children's lives everyday and take no thought of it. Many do jobs which are dangerous and life-threatening. They do these heartily and without a second thought. However, when it comes to the work of God, the risks seem to be too high! Giving yourself wholly to God includes giving your life to the Master even if you lose it.

Chapter 18

The Mysterious Purposes of Full-Time Ministry

It is time to magnify full-time ministry. I have magnified the lay ministry for years and many have taken that road. As Paul said,

> **But I am speaking to you who are Gentiles. Inasmuch then as I am an apostle of Gentiles, I magnify my ministry**
>
> **Romans 11:13**

Paul made his ministry important by stressing on it and teaching about it.

> **As you know, God has appointed me as a special messenger to you Gentiles. I lay great stress on this and remind the Jews about it as often as I can,**
>
> **Romans 11:13, TLB**

It is important to magnify the ministry. Full-time ministry is important. It is the priesthood. It is the fulfilling of the call of God. Full-time ministers are the New Testament Levites. Full-time ministry is mysterious in that it is not easy to perceive or even faintly quantify what a priest does to occupy himself all day long and everyday of the year.

Yet, it is the highest calling and the most important work that a person could be involved in. I can confirm this to be a reality.

This section of the book will help you to understand some of the hidden purposes, which are accomplished through full-time ministry.

Because of the mystique surrounding the work of a priest, little is known about it. That is why I am writing this book.

1. Enter full-time ministry to avoid the neglect of your gift.

NEGLECT NOT the gift that is in thee...

1 Timothy 4:14

Many gifts will be neglected until you give yourself wholly to them! Because these gifts are spiritual, it is not easy to see that they are being neglected. This is one of the reasons why God is calling you to full-time ministry. He wants you to have time to attend to the spiritual gifts and callings on your life.

The first thing I noticed when I entered full-time ministry was how free I was to travel to plant churches and to do the work of God. Without being in full-time ministry, I would not have been able to attend to the work of planting churches. There is no secular job that would accommodate my absence from work for such long periods. It may not be apparent to you, but many things are neglected because people do not give themselves wholly to the ministry.

So Busy in Ministry

One of the mysterious things about my full-time staff is that they are so busy and have hardly any time for anything else. It makes you wonder about what was happening to the issues they attend to now. Obviously, those things were being neglected until they came along to attend to them fully.

One medical doctor now in full-time ministry remarked, "I am so busy now and I have no time for anything else."

He continued, "Yet, a year ago I was equally busy running my hospital."

He said, "It's amazing. There is so much work to be done and I was busy elsewhere."

You see, God's work lies largely undone and neglected. God is calling many to come into His service and do His work and nothing else.

Is There Anything to Do?

When you are a layperson, the largeness of the work to be done is not apparent. Somehow, it is not obvious from the layman's point of view. That is why newcomers to full-time ministry, who have laboured in banks, hospitals, companies, etc., are genuinely surprised to find themselves inundated with work, which they cannot finish. They are simply amazed at how they are continually exhausted with work which never ends.

I smiled to myself when a lay brother said to me, "Of course I will come to work in the ministry if there is something to do." There is something to do indeed! The whole world is waiting for us to come to them.

God has sent us to tell six billion people about Jesus. Do you think that that is a lot of work? I do, and I think there is a lot of work for as many as are willing.

A song I love says,

There are so many jobs in God's vineyard for all of us to do.
The harvest is plentiful but the labourers are few
There are so many jobs in God's vineyard for all of us to do
We must work while it is day spreading the Word of God
As we walk along the way
We live to do His will, spreading the Word of God
Till it reaches to every hill.
We must witness to everyone we meet in every song we sing
We must tell them of the soon coming King
We must witness to everyone we meet in every song we sing
We must tell them of the soon coming King.

God called me to be a pastor and a teacher. I could have neglected that gift and spent my days doing something else. For the last several years, I have given attention to my calling. Indeed, it has been several years of growing in the anointing and gifting of the Lord.

2. Full-time ministry is for meditation, reading, exhortation.

Till I come, give attendance to reading, to exhortation, to doctrine.

1 Timothy 4:13

Many people do not even understand the purpose for which they are in full-time ministry. One of the principal reasons for full-time ministry is meditation, reading and exhortation. Each of these activities is different and has a unique place.

Reading

When you work in the secular world there is little time for reading. A minister is someone who must be "given" to reading. Reading is one of the most important activities of someone called to full-time ministry.

Reading the Bible and reading other books takes a lot of time and has no substitute. Unfortunately, many who are in full-time ministry do not do the very thing for which they became full-time ministers. Forgive!

Reading is not regarded as work. It is generally seen as something to be done in one's leisure. Sadly, many pastors do not understand that reading is their God-given work. As you read, you go deeper into the things of God. Your depth determines the height you can climb to.

I have found reading to be even more important than praying. Reading has opened doors for me and lifted me to new heights in ministry.

Meditation

The church is filled with ministers who glance briefly at Scriptures and read over large portions rapidly. That is why there is a lack of personal revelation. Sermons are empty and there is no depth in what is being said. Instead of spending hours meditating, ministers love to repeat and relay the revelations of others who have sought God and meditated on His Word.

Meditation is thinking deeply about God's Word. Indeed, the lack of meditation is the cause of a lack of personal conviction.

Both Kenneth Hagin and Rick Joyner have had powerful visions. I love reading their visions and benefiting spiritually from them. I long for visions from the Lord that will teach me precious hidden truths. However, I cannot spend my whole life waiting for a vision, I have to do what all ministers are supposed to do - meditation.

Sometimes people have visions that are deep revelations about the Word. God gives these supernatural blessings. However, most of us will not have these special revelations. We will have to depend on meditation. I can always tell when I speak to someone who meditates on the Word of God. He is full of wisdom and understanding. It is dangerous to relay the messages of others without taking the time to meditate for yourself. You could easily become a false prophet reading out dead sermons whose relevance have expired.

Exhortation

Exhortation is all about sharing the Word with one another. I love to share the Word with anybody who loves the Word. It is sweet like honey and tasty like spicy, grilled pork chops. It is such a delight for me to share wonderful truths with small groups and individuals.

What people do not realize is that, as you share, you become more grounded in the truth. You understand and remember the Word better. Exhortation helps you to preach better. That is why exhortation is important for full-time ministers. Just like reading and meditation, it grooms you for your ministry.

3. **Full-time ministry is to ensure salvation.**

   ...for in doing this thou shalt both SAVE THYSELF, and them that hear thee.

   1 Timothy 4:16

Take pains with these things; be absorbed in them, so that your progress will be evident to all. Pay close attention to yourself and to your teaching; persevere in these things, for as you do this you will ENSURE SALVATION both for yourself and for those who hear you.

1 Timothy 4:15-16, NASB

One of the mysterious purposes of full-time ministry is to ensure salvation and to save yourself. How can that be? If God has called you to ministry, it would be dangerous to do anything else. Paul said, "Woe is me if I preach not the gospel". He also said, "necessity is laid upon me". In other words, it is very necessary that I preach the Word.

If your boss sent for you, wouldn't you go? If you did not go when you were called what would happen? He is likely to dismiss you for refusing to come when called. That is why servants are quick to respond and ready to do anything. Servants want to keep their jobs and their lives.

There are people who have died prematurely because they refused to give themselves wholly to God's calling.

Years ago, a young man said to me, "God has called me to ministry. I want to be in full-time ministry."

But I told him, "There is no opportunity for you to work in the ministry at this time."

But he insisted, "If I don't work for the Lord in full-time ministry, I feel that I will die."

"Wow," I said. "I know that feeling."

I allowed him to be in full-time ministry and today he has a great church and ministry.

"Woe is me" simply means something terrible will happen to me. You see, the genuine call of God leaves you with no options. Who are you to refuse God's outstretched hand?

Do you know the One who has called you? He is El Shaddai, the Almighty God.

Do You Dare Disobey This Call?

Jonah experienced the terror of rejecting the call of God. Rejecting the call to full-time ministry will only provoke the storms of life and prepare the whales in the sea to receive you.

By rejecting the call of God, Jonah walked right into the storms of life. He fell into the hands of wicked men who heartlessly threw him overboard.

As if that was not enough, he was swallowed by a big fish and stayed in the belly of the fish for some days.

Finally, he was vomited out and given a second chance to obey the call of God.

Now the word of the LORD came to Jonah the SECOND TIME, saying, "Arise, go to Nineveh the great city and proclaim to it the proclamation which I am going to tell you.

Jonah 3:1-2, NASB

Expect storms and expect wicked people to take over your life if you disobey the Master. God controls everything.

When Jonah had a bad attitude, the Lord appointed a plant to cover him and then sent a worm to eat the plant. God also sent the wind to Jonah. This illustrates the almighty power of the One who calls us.

So the LORD God appointed a plant and it grew up over Jonah to be a shade over his head to deliver him from his discomfort. And Jonah was extremely happy about the plant.

But God appointed a worm when dawn came the next day and it attacked the plant and it withered.

When the sun came up God appointed a scorching east wind, and the sun beat down on Jonah's head so that

he became faint and begged with all his soul to die, saying, "Death is better to me than life."

Jonah 4:6-8, NASB

Even the growing of a plant and the movement of a worm are determined by God. I believe there are many people whose lives are ruined because they failed to come into full-time ministry. Their lives are ruined because they could not trust and obey God. Sadly, some people even lose their salvation by running away from full-time ministry. This is why Paul said giving yourself wholly would ensure salvation. Our very lives depend on obeying God. You can make light of God's call, but you may pay dearly for it.

4. Full-time ministry sets a good example.

...that thy profiting may APPEAR TO ALL.

1 Timothy 4:15

Several good examples are set when you enter full-time ministry. You set an example of faith and of trusting in God. Full-time ministry sets an example of loving God and obeying Him. Full-time ministry demonstrates that you believe in the sacrifice of the cross. You have taken up your cross and are following the Saviour.

Full-time ministry sets a good example of implementing the Scriptures practically. It makes you a doer of the Word.

Interestingly, we cannot relate with large sections of the Scriptures unless the model of full-time ministry is practised.

Many of the truths relating to the tabernacle, the Levites and the priests have no relevance to people who do not practise the complete dedication that full-time ministry requires.

Many things that Paul said about the ministry relate to people who are completely immersed in ministry.

Many of his struggles and teachings are from the perspective of someone completely dedicated to the service of God. Even the often-quoted Scripture, "My God shall supply all your needs" had to do with him receiving support in full-time ministry.

The famous verse in Galatians 6:7 about reaping what you sow is also related to him receiving financial support for full-time ministry.

5. Full-time ministry permits the continuation of your ministry.

Take heed unto thyself, and unto the doctrine; CONTINUE IN THEM...

1 Timothy 4:16

Many people practise a part-time ministry, giving God some weekends and some evenings of their lives. This is all well and good and sometimes is a necessary phase of ministry.

However, full-time ministry is a logical continuation of the lay ministry. What you have done for years on a part-time basis can be continued and upgraded in full-time ministry. It is indeed a privilege to have the opportunity to continue to fulfil your call at a higher level. If God has called you to the ministry, pray for the opportunity to go all the way. I have experienced both lay ministry and full-time ministry. I can tell you, it is the greatest blessing to give yourself wholly to the Lord.

6. Full-time ministry is for the protection of yourself and your message.

TAKE HEED unto THYSELF, and UNTO THE DOCTRINE; continue in them...

1 Timothy 4:16

An ambassador is a special envoy with a special message. Every minister is an ambassador.

Now then we are ambassadors for Christ, as though God did beseech you by us: we pray you in Christ's stead, be ye reconciled to God.

2 Corinthians 5:20

It is important that a messenger does not change the message he was given. The messenger himself must not be corrupted or swayed by the people. He must be faithful to the one who sent him.

Recently, I needed to send a message to someone. The message was a very hard message of judgment. I did not want to do it myself so I looked for a messenger. Somehow, I knew that each of the people I was thinking of would modify the message.

They would say things differently and tone the message down.

Then I got discouraged and gave up the idea of delivering that message. I understood why God had said, "Who will go for me?" I began to identify with God's problem of finding a faithful, reliable messenger who would deliver the truth without compromise. Unfortunately, the very sight of the recipients of the message frightens the messengers and they come up with amazing variants of the original.

In full-time ministry, spending more time with the Lord ensures that you protect the doctrine and the message given to you. It is easy to deliver a mutant of the original message.

I believe that much of what is preached currently is a mutation of God's Word. Because Scriptures and Bibles are used in the pulpit, innocent and ignorant people swallow the modified messages of the modern church.

Listening to present-day preaching would leave any genuine student of the Bible wondering. Rick Joyner, in his vision of the *Final Quest* described how he met the apostle Paul. He asked Paul for any comments he had about the church. Paul had one comment. He said he could not recognize the message nor the ministry of the present-day church. Paul said the message of the first church was the message of the cross and that message had been quickly lost by the church. How sad!

I am not surprised that Paul cannot recognize what we are preaching. Many messages centre on the felt needs of people. These felt needs in Christian parlance are called blessings -

things that people feel, need and want. Things like money, cars, houses, children, visas, jobs, wives, husbands and how to acquire them, take centre stage of most teachings.

In addition, many messages sound like good advice for successful living. Most of the preaching has very little divine and mystical content.

Where are the sermons on salvation and the blood of Jesus? What about the cross, Heaven and Hell? Can we even preach about sacrifice in this lukewarm Laodecian church? What about eternity and the power of God?

Full-time ministry is intended to give you time for attending to God and His Word. A full-time ministry of meditation, Bible study, waiting on God and praying, will help us to protect the message and the doctrine of the church.

Chapter 19

The Principles behind
Full-Time Ministry

One of the barriers to full-time ministry is the guilt that comes from earning money from a church. Acquiring any kind of benefit for working in a church seems almost sinful to many traditional Christians. A guilty feeling that you are living off the gifts that people bring to God can be overwhelming.

Many well-meaning Christians find it virtually impossible to cross this barrier and to work for the Lord in full-time ministry. This guilty feeling is not unfounded. Even though a bank is a heartless, money-grabbing institution, earning or getting some of that money for yourself by working there is seen as legitimate.

Somehow, earning money through the church seems immoral. It is therefore a struggle for professionals to subject themselves to earning money from a charity, which they once contributed to.

Generally, coming into full-time ministry is a humbling experience. It must be embraced by all who love the Lord. The apostle Paul throws much light on what happens when you earn money through the ministry.

He teaches powerful principles which every full-time minister must understand. Even lay people must understand these principles. They help put everything in context.

These principles are fulfilled by being in full-time ministry, that is, a ministry which pays you or from which you benefit financially. These principles are not fulfilled by lay ministry.

You must not feel guilty about receiving pay or benefits through ministry work. All these ten principles are in favour of you receiving money and other benefits from your work.

Ten Guilt Removing Principles

1. The principle of fighting a war whilst someone else pays the bills.

Who at any time serves as a soldier at his own expense?

1 Corinthians 9:7, NASB

Paul likens ministry to going to war. Indeed, it is a battle on many fronts. After being in full-time ministry for more than ten years, I would describe ministry as a series of battles, struggles and fights.

If I am at war through the ministry, who is going to pay for the war? Certainly not the soldiers who are fighting on the battle front!

If you are in full-time ministry, you can expect to be paid for going to war. Actually, you should expect to be paid well! You are in a danger zone and have taken many risks.

2. The principle of being the first to drink the wine of your vineyard.

...Who plants a vineyard and does not eat the fruit of it?

1 Corinthians 9:7, NASB

In this verse, the work of the ministry is likened to the planting and tilling of a vineyard. This principle gives the planter of the vineyard the right to enjoy the wine that comes from his vineyard. The next time you are offered a cup of wine from the ministry vineyard, do not feel guilty to drink it. Drink deeply, brother. You deserve the wine from the vineyard.

3. The principle of not muzzling the ox that treads out the corn.

For it is written in the Law of Moses, "You shall not muzzle the ox while he is threshing..."

1 Corinthians 9:9, NASB

In this principle, the mouth of the ox, which is treading the corn, must not be gagged! The ox spends the whole day mashing the corn for its master. The mouth of this ox must not be tied. The ox must be allowed to eat some of the corn he is stamping on. How much corn can this poor animal eat in a day?

Now, God does not use this principle because He cares about oxen! He cares about His full-time priests.

A full-time pastor is an ox who spends all day crushing the corn for the farmer. He is entitled to a few mouthfuls to give him enough energy to continue happily in his work.

Dear Minister, you are also entitled to enjoy a few mouthfuls personally. Don't feel bad because you have to eat. It is God's blessing for you.

4. The principle of feeding a flock and being the first to drink the milk.

...Or who tends a flock and does not use the milk of the flock?

1 Corinthians 9:7, NASB

Once again, a full-time minister feeds the flock as he ministers the Word of God. These sheep are definitely going to get fatter. They will be blessed and increased in size and number. Soon milk will start coming out of those teats.

Who should be the first to drink this milk? You are abnormal when you do not drink the milk from your sheep.

Feel free from today and enjoy the milk! Put it in the fridge if you want. Have a cup of tea with this God-given milk. You may turn the milk into cheese, butter, yoghurt, ice cream and all the other nice things. I know you never thought that God would bless you so much in full-time ministry.

5. The principle of having a farm and eating of the produce.

Yes, for our sake it was written, because the plowman ought to plow in hope, and the thresher to thresh in hope of sharing the crops.

1 Corinthians 9:10, NASB

Pastoring a church is like owning a farm. Think of all the cows, pigs, goats, chickens, wheat, barley, maize, potatoes, oranges, bananas, tomatoes, pepper and onions that are grown on your farm. Being in full-time ministry is the same as having all these at your disposal.

Is it wrong to taste spicy, grilled pork chops once a week? Is there anything wrong if you use some of the tomatoes, pepper and onions to make chicken stew for your family? What about some steak or beef with onions? How do you want your potatoes? As french fries, parsley potatoes or baked potatoes?

These are God's blessings for his full-time ministers. It is a small compensation for the humility and service of a servant of God. No one is wiser than God. Accept God's provision and flow fully in full-time ministry. Enjoy the fried rice that comes from the farm.

6. The principle of sowing spiritual seeds and reaping material things.

If we sowed spiritual things in you, is it too much if we reap material things from you?
If others share the right over you, do we not more? Nevertheless, we did not use this right, but we endure all things so that we will cause no hindrance to the gospel of Christ.

1 Corinthians 9:11-12, NASB

The ministry is all about sowing spiritual seeds. I would have thought that the harvest would be equally spiritual. However, God's Word reveals this surprise of carnal blessings as well. What are carnal blessings? They are physical things that you receive only on this earth. There is nothing carnal in Heaven. Eternal rewards await you in Heaven but carnal harvests may be reaped here and now. People should not be surprised when God blesses full-time ministers with cars, houses, clothes, food and other little carnal pleasures.

Unfortunately, there are many who want us to sow and never reap. There are lay people who cannot understand why they should pay the bills for the war which we are fighting. Well, that is God's ordained way.

7. The principle of ministering holy things and living off these holy things.

Do you not know that those who perform sacred services eat the food of the temple...

1 Corinthians 9:13, NASB

Full-time ministry is based on the levitical priesthood. All the tribes of Israel were given land but the tribe of Levi was given nothing. Their portion was the Lord. They were to trust God for everything.

The priests the Levites, and all the tribe of Levi, shall have no part nor inheritance with Israel: THEY SHALL EAT THE OFFERINGS of the LORD made by fire, and his inheritance.

Therefore shall they have no inheritance among their brethren: the LORD is their inheritance, as he hath said unto them. And THIS SHALL BE THE PRIEST'S DUE FROM THE PEOPLE, from them that offer a sacrifice, whether it be ox or sheep; and they shall give unto the priest the shoulder, and the two cheeks, and the maw.

THE FIRSTFRUIT also of thy corn, of thy wine, and of thine oil, and the first of the fleece of thy sheep, SHALT THOU GIVE HIM. For the LORD thy God hath chosen him out of all thy tribes, to stand to minister in the name of the LORD, him and his sons for ever.

Deuteronomy 18:1-5

So practically, they were to receive the tithes, offerings, and gifts on behalf of the Lord. After presenting these gifts to the Lord with a wave, they were to take them home and enjoy them.

It might seem like sacrilege to you, for me to eat people's offerings! How can someone eat and drink holy gifts that have been presented to God? How could I use money that was placed in the Sunday offering bowl? Nevertheless, it is a principle that those who minister with holy things are to eat and to drink these very holy things. Because I am in full-time ministry, I use holy money, I drink holy milk with my tea and I eat holy beef stew.

Why do I call it holy? Because I eat the offerings and tithes that people have brought. I use these offerings and tithes to buy food and drink.

Next time you see a full-time minister spending a dollar, remember that it is a holy dollar that he is spending.

All full-time ministers spend holy money and eat holy food. They drive holy cars and live in holy houses because all these were acquired with holy offerings! I am sorry I cannot change what God has ordained.

8. The principle of waiting at the altar and partaking of the altar.

...those who attend regularly to the altar have their share from the altar?

1 Corinthians 9:13, NASB

The principle of partaking of things brought to the altar is similar to the one above. God's people bring tithes, offerings and gifts to His house. In the Old Testament, these altar sacrifices were sheep, oxen, chicken, etc. After receiving the gifts, the priests presented them on the altar.

After church, we take these gifts to our homes and share them. Sometimes there are larger portions of beef and this is good for khebab! Sometimes there are many chickens and that can be used for chicken soup, grilled chicken and other delicacies that the Levitical children love!

Things presented on the altar are sacred and belong to God. We do not eat these sacrifices with presumption. We see it as an honour from the Lord. It is His way of looking after His priests.

It is truly humbling to own nothing except that which comes from people's gifts. Everyone can point to your house and say that it is not earned by "honest work".

But God sees His priests as hard-working men and women who deserve to be rewarded. The work they do is more than "honest work". It is God's work!!

9. The principle of eating and drinking as you work.

Do we not have a right to eat and drink?

1 Corinthians 9:4, NASB

It is important to eat and drink as you work. When people do not eat and drink as they work, they grow weary and give up. Can you imagine having to fast every day of your life just because you work at a particular place? Why should full-time ministers not eat whilst they work?

10. The principle of taking a break from work.

Or do only Barnabas and I not have a right to refrain from working?

1 Corinthians 9:6, NASB

How can someone work without ever resting? Rest is part of God's plan for His cherished ministers. God wants full-time ministers to have vacations, days off and times of rest. It is their right. Please do not feel bad to have a day off. In my church we have Mondays off. It is our resting day and it is our little time of leisure and family respite from our work.

Shouldn't I Play Golf?

One Monday, I was on the golf course with some other pastors. A gentleman who did not know that my associate pastor was tying his shoe laces behind him, began to criticize me.

He said, "If that guy was working as a doctor, would he be playing golf here today?"

My pastor reacted to his comments and challenged him about what he was saying.

He told him, "We are all gentlemen on the course. What do you mean by what you are saying? Respect yourself!"

"You are a grown up!" he was told sharply.

We asked the man whether he was paying for us to play golf. The man sputtered out a lame response, claiming to enjoy my radio programs. Quite irritated, we decided to ignore this fellow and to carry on with our game.

But this is the question Paul was asking. "Or I only and Barnabas, have not we power to forbear working?" (1 Corinthians 9:6).

People feel that they have the right "to forbear working" and to have days off, vacations, and times of relaxation. But they see no reason why a priest should have the same privileges.

The Response of Apostle Paul

This is my answer to those who question my rights.

Or don't I have any rights at all? Can't I claim the same privilege the other apostles have of being a guest in your homes?

If I had a wife, and if she were a believer, couldn't I bring her along on these trips just as the other disciples do, and as the Lord's brothers do, and as Peter does?

And must Barnabas and I alone keep working for our living while you supply these others?

What soldier in the army has to pay his own expenses? And have you ever heard of a farmer who harvests his crop and doesn't have the right to eat some of it? What shepherd takes care of a flock of sheep and goats and isn't allowed to drink some of the milk?

And I'm not merely quoting the opinions of men as to what is right. I'm telling you what God's law says.

For in the law God gave to Moses he said that you must not put a muzzle on an ox to keep it from eating when it is treading out the wheat. Do you suppose God was thinking only about oxen when he said this?

Wasn't he also thinking about us? Of course he was. He said this to show us that Christian workers should be paid by those they help. Those who do the plowing and threshing should expect some share of the harvest.

We have planted good spiritual seed in your souls. Is it too much to ask, in return, for mere food and clothing?

You give them to others who preach to you, and you should. But shouldn't we have an even greater right to them? Yet we have never used this right but supply our own needs without your help. We have never demanded payment of any kind for fear that, if we did, you might be less interested in our message to you from Christ.

Don't you realize that God told those working in his temple to take for their own needs some of the food brought there as gifts to him? And those who work at the altar of God get a share of the food that is brought by those offering it to the Lord.

In the same way the Lord has given orders that those who preach the Gospel should be supported by those who accept it.

1 Corinthians 9:3-14, TLB

Chapter 20

Wrong Reasons for Full-Time Ministry

...the LORD looks at the heart.

1 Samuel 16:7, NASB

It is important that you have right motives. God looks at the heart. You are dealing with someone who does not care what you say or what impressions you make. He looks straight at your heart. There are many possible reasons for doing the same thing. If you are genuine, you will always question your heart. You will search and check constantly to see if any corruption has seeped in.

Almost every aspect of the ministry has a list of wrong reasons that motivate ministers. For instance, there are many wrong reasons for wanting to have a big church. You may desire power and fame. You may love the praises of men.

You may do evangelism and feed the poor but your motive may again be fame. You may be motivated by your own human compassion for poverty and disease and not by the inspiration of the Holy Spirit.

You may preach powerful messages on the financial harvest. You will say it is because you want the people to prosper. You may say Jesus spoke more about money than anything else. You may say, "God told me to speak these words." But the real reason may be that you simply want a good offering for that service! Mercy!

As I grow in the Lord, I have noticed an increasing uncertainty in me about everything I do. Every genuine minister will suffer some amount of confusion because of a constant searching of his heart.

Why are you doing what you are doing? Has God called you? What is in your heart? What is the real reason for what you are saying? We are rapidly approaching Heaven and the throne of judgement. Nothing about us will be hidden.

Everything will be laid bare before the King of Kings. Our evil motives will be even uglier when exposed to the glory of God. It is time to search our hearts and judge ourselves so that God will not have to do it. As the psalmist said,

Search me, O God, and know my heart: try me, and know my thoughts: And see if there be any wicked way in me, and lead me in the way everlasting.

Psalm 139:23

Can there be wrong reasons for entering into full-time ministry? Certainly! Many wrong reasons and motives hide in the hearts of priests. It is important to know these and make sure you have the right motive for ministry.

Wrong Reasons for Entering Full-Time Ministry

1. I could desire to be in full-time ministry because I did not do well in school and I am not qualified for any other profession.

2. My desire to be in full-time ministry could be because people in full-time ministry look prosperous.

3. My desire to be in full-time ministry could be because those in full-time ministry travel abroad often.

4. I could desire to be in full-time ministry because I am currently unemployed.

5. I could desire to be in full-time ministry because it is a better paying job than my current one.

6. I could desire to be in full-time ministry because I need a stepping stone to that which I really want to do.

7. I could be in full-time ministry because my spouse pressured me into it.

8. I could be in full-time ministry because I need to work in a family-oriented organization during my childbearing years.

9. I could desire to be in full-time ministry because I am too lazy to look for another job.

10. I could be in full-time ministry because I have earned all the money and acquired everything I will ever need so I now feel secure enough to work for God.

11. I could be in full-time ministry because I do not want to look unspiritual and uncommitted.

12. I could be in full-time ministry because I think I will have a job with a lighter schedule.

These are just a few of the wrong reasons why someone could desire to be in full-time ministry. Please check your heart and make sure that you are in full-time ministry for the right reason.

Chapter 21

Right Reasons for Full-Time Ministry

1. Enter full-time ministry because you love God.

…the greatest of these is love.

1 Corinthians 13:13, NASB

There are many good reasons for someone to be in full-time ministry, but the greatest of these is love.

Believing and obeying a command from God is a very good motive for doing something. However, the greatest of motives is love. Going into full-time ministry with hope for eternal or earthly rewards is also a good thing. After all, you must believe that God is a rewarder of them that diligently seek Him. However, an even greater motive is the motivation of love.

I realize that my reason for serving God has gradually shifted from doing things because I need to obey His calling to doing things because I love Him. And that is a major shift!

Choosing the Best of Three

If I had to choose between three employees: one who was very qualified, one who was very experienced and one who simply loved and believed in me, I would choose the one who loved me.

Peter Worked for Love

Peter loved Jesus. That was the basis of all the work that he did. The ministry of the apostles was not for money or fame. The money lover (Judas) was kicked out at the beginning of the ministry. Jesus capitalized on Peter's love and urged him on in the ministry.

> **So when they had finished breakfast, Jesus said to Simon Peter, "Simon, son of John, do you love Me more than these?" He said to Him, "Yes, Lord; You know that I love You." He said to him, "Tend My lambs."**
>
> **He said to him again a second time, "Simon, son of John, do you love Me?" He said to Him, "Yes, Lord; You know that I love You." He said to him, "Shepherd My sheep."**
>
> **He said to him the third time, "Simon, son of John, do you love Me?" Peter was grieved because He said to him the third time, "Do you love Me?" And he said to Him, "Lord, You know all things; You know that I love You." Jesus said to him, "Tend My sheep."**
>
>

John 21:15-17, NASB

Paul Worked for Love

Paul was constrained by his love for Christ. He was not just a hard worker trying to achieve many things at the same time. He loved the Saviour!

> **For the love of Christ constraineth us...**
>
>

2 Corinthians 5:14

2. Enter full-time ministry because you fear God.

> **For if I preach the gospel, I have nothing to boast of, for necessity is laid upon me; yes, woe is me if I do not preach the gospel!**
>
>

1 Corinthians 9:16, NKJV

Elijah said to Elisha, "What have I done to you?" He knew that by throwing the mantle on him he had changed the young man's life forever. He had no options. He had to go. If he did not obey the call, there would be plenty of trouble. Jonah found out first-hand what it meant to run away from the call of God. His troubles never ended until he obeyed the call.

Come into full-time ministry now because you have no other options! One of the great problems of modern Christians is a lack of the fear of God. You can detect that there is little fear of God by the way Christians treat God's representatives. When Miriam criticized Moses, the Lord asked her, "Were you not afraid to speak against my servant?

Why then were you not afraid to speak against My servant, against Moses?"

Numbers 12:8

3. Enter full-time ministry to fulfil your calling.

...make full proof of thy ministry

2 Timothy 4:5

Do not die without discharging all your duties. Do not leave anything undone! Many ministries cannot be fulfilled until you do it on a full-time basis! You will not live for long. That is not a curse. It is the truth! Your days are numbered and so are mine.

We have a very short time in which to finish our work. How sad it will be if you get to Heaven and find out that you could have done much more with your ministry.

As with everything, if you give yourself wholly to it, it will blossom. Another version says "...Leave nothing undone that you ought to do" (2 Timothy 4:5, TLB). Yet another version puts it this way, "...discharge all the duties of your ministry" (2 Timothy 4:5, NIV).

4. Enter full-time ministry to finish your work.

I have fought the good fight, I HAVE FINISHED THE COURSE, I have kept the faith;

2 Timothy 4:7

A Visit from the Dead

I had a vision in which I found myself sitting at a dining table with two dead pastors who had come back to life for a short period. The men, who were brothers, had died years ago and had been brought back to life and given a chance to revisit the earth.

Whilst on this short visit they had gone around some churches that they had established in their lifetime and tried to minister to them.

We Talked

I was privileged, in the vision, to have a meal with them before they returned to be with the Lord. Actually, my home was the last place they were visiting on earth. As we ate and shared fellowship, I asked them a few questions.

"How was your stay on earth and how did you find the churches?"

They shook their heads and said, "Our messages did not work. They seemed irrelevant to the people. No one wanted to listen to us."

He continued, "Our songs also did not work. No one wanted to sing them. They had new songs and were not interested in our old songs."

They seemed discouraged and disappointed that they had made no impact at all.

They Warned Me

I asked, "Is there anything you would like to share with me before you leave?"

One of them answered, "There are some things that we would like to tell you. First of all, we were very surprised to die when we died! We never expected to have died when we did. You see, we were very fruitful and active in the ministry. Of course, we thought that this was a good reason for us to live much longer. Why would God remove someone who was doing so well in ministry?"

He continued, "The second thing is that even though we tried to influence people during this visit, the people were not impressed by our ministry at all. We had no impact at all."

Then he turned, pointed to me and said, "You have the best chance now. This is your time to be fruitful. Our time is past. Our chance is gone. This is your best chance now."

The vision ended and I realized that God had spoken to me. It was clear that I could depart from this earth at any time in spite of what good works I was doing. God had told me that this was my chance to do His will and to finish His work.

Dear brother, this is our best chance. Soon you will be out of this world. You will not have a chance to work for God. Why do you want to serve Him in drips and drops? Throw fear and caution to the wind. Launch out into full-time ministry and give God your best. This is your best chance now. Make sure you finish your course.

5. Enter full-time ministry to be able to travel.

In journeyings often...

2 Corinthians 11:26

Ministry involves a lot of travelling. The souls Christ died for are not in one place. They are scattered all over the surface of the earth. They are found in cities, towns and villages dotted all over the world. We can never fulfil God's calling by staying in one place. We must go, we must travel, and we must spread out our wings and fly!

When you work for secular institutions, you will not be able to travel freely. Every normal job will restrict and restrain you from true ministry. Enter full-time ministry so that you can travel to where God sends you.

6. Enter full-time ministry to be able to be sent.

And Tychicus I have sent to Ephesus.

2 Timothy 4:12, NKJV

How can you be sent if you are tied down to a particular job? Your boss will dismiss you for absenteeism. This is the first thing that I realized when I entered full-time ministry. I was free to be sent. The Lord could send me anywhere, any day.

Here am I, send me! We sing it but it is not real. How can you be sent to the villages and towns when you have to report to the bank at 8.00am???

7. Enter full-time ministry to be able to live at certain places.

For this cause LEFT I THEE IN CRETE, that thou shouldest set in order the things that are wanting, and ordain elders in every city, as I had appointed thee:

Titus 1:5

I have left several young men in different towns of the world.

How could I leave them there to "set in order things that are wanting" if they had to be at work on Wednesday morning? The young men that I have left in different towns are called missionaries. Paul sent Titus as a missionary to Crete. How can you be a missionary when you have to go to work in the bank every morning?

8. Enter full-time ministry because you despise earthly things.

Yea doubtless, and I count all things but loss for the excellency of the knowledge of Christ Jesus my Lord: for whom I have suffered the loss of all things, and do count them but dung, that I may win Christ,

Philippians 3:8

It is sad to see Christians aspiring to join the ranks of the world's great. Pastors want to be numbered among society's elite. We love to take pictures with earthly presidents and to be associated with rich people. Forgive!

Somehow, rich worldly people are the best friends of many pastors! What do they talk about? That spirit of worldliness in ministers is transmitted to the church.

Our churches are filled with people who are in awe of this world! If they were heavenly-minded they would be despising the world.

How different we are from the Apostle Paul. Paul considered these things as dung and we consider them as glamorous treasures. Heaven cannot relate with our strange desires for things that fade so easily.

It is time to put everything in its right place. Every earthly achievement is dung in the light of the glory of God.

Spiritual men must despise the riches, the accomplishments and the prestige of this world.

For all flesh is as grass, and all the GLORY OF MAN AS THE FLOWER OF GRASS. The grass withereth, and the flower thereof falleth away...

1 Peter 1:24

It is time to set your affection on things above.

Set your affection on things above, not on things on the earth.

Colossians 3:2

Falling in love with full-time ministry is setting your affection on things above. The rewards of serving God can be found in Heaven where our hearts and minds should be.

9. Enter full-time ministry to be able to fight a good war.

No man that warreth entangleth himself with the affairs of this life; that he may please him who hath chosen him to be a soldier.

2 Timothy 2:4

Ministry is war! To fight a war well, you need soldiers that are committed to fighting. Soldiers cannot go shopping when they want to. The American soldiers in Iraq cannot go to their old jobs in Houston, Texas. They cannot go shopping in the beautiful shopping malls of America. They cannot go to McDonald's or watch films in the evenings with their girlfriends. They have to watch out for bombs. They cannot fight the Iraqis from their comfortable and safe positions in America. They have to go away from their comforts and luxuries and join the battle. They will risk their lives and everything they have ever known for the sake of their mission.

That is how full-time ministry is. You have to leave behind the old life with its routine and launch out into a completely different life. *Come into full-time ministry so that you can fight the war properly.*

10. Enter full-time ministry because of the rewards in Heaven.

There are many rewards for God's servants. I am looking forward to mine and I hope you have yours.

> **Peter began to say to Him, "Behold, we have left everything and followed You."**
>
> **Jesus said, "Truly I say to you, there is no one who has left house or brothers or sisters or mother or father or children or farms, for My sake and for the gospel's sake, but that he will receive a hundred times as much now in the present age, houses and brothers and sisters and mothers and children and farms, along with persecutions; and in the age to come, eternal life."**
>
> **Mark 10:28-30, NASB**

Chapter 22

How to Assess Your Readiness for Full-Time Ministry

As you get ready for the challenge of full-time ministry, you must ask yourself some questions. You must go through some issues in your heart and settle them forever.

Full-time ministry is not about finding a new job. It is not a career move. There are many better-paying jobs elsewhere. Full-time ministry is all about following God into the unknown. It is a walk of faith and faith is all about "things not seen". I want to take you through a series of questions that you must ask yourself before you embark on something as challenging as full-time ministry.

Ten Questions to Ask Yourself Before Full-Time Ministry

1. Are you ready to leave familiar things behind?

Now the LORD said to Abram, Go forth from...your relatives

Genesis 12:1, NASB

Are you ready to leave your old friends and acquaintances behind? Do they mean so much to you that you cannot do without them? I assure you that being in full-time ministry separates you from many familiar things. In full-time ministry your day off is usually on Monday. Most secular workers are at work on Monday morning. This reality will separate you from lay people and their lives.

2. Are you ready to leave your own country?

Now the LORD said to Abram, Go forth from your country,

Genesis 12:1, NASB

It would appear that there is little need for full-time ministers. This seems to be the picture if we do not travel to other countries on Gospel missions. God's command is for us to go to the uttermost parts of the earth. Thousands of full-time ministers are needed for the great commission.

If we are ready to go to the nations, there will never be enough people for full-time ministry. Ask yourself therefore, if you are ready to leave your country, region or neighbourhood. Going away from your country is a real option for anyone coming into full-time ministry.

3. Are you ready to break away from your father's influence and provision?

Now the LORD said to Abram...Go forth from...your father's house,

Genesis 12:1, NASB

Are you ready to leave the influence of your home? Can you be free from your father's influence, control and money? One day a prophet told me about a revelation he had had. It was about one of our lay pastors who had declined to come into full-time ministry.

The Vision

In the vision, this pastor was seen depending on his father to give him certain things like money, houses, inheritance, etc. This pastor did not want to do anything that would upset his father and so he rejected the offer to come into full-time ministry. In the vision, the father died but did not give his son any of the things he was expecting. The brother was very disappointed. He had sacrificed full-time ministry for an earthly inheritance that never materialized! How sad!

You see, you must be ready to leave your father's house and all its good things. They are all "dung" compared to the riches and rewards that Christ has for you.

4. Are you ready for uncertainty?

Now the LORD said to Abram, Go forth from…to the land which I will show you;

Genesis 12:1, NASB

I get amused when people want to know details of what full-time ministry involves. They want to know what the offer is. Someone said his career progression in the ministry was not clear. Would he rise quickly from Zonal Pastor to Sub-District Pastor to District Pastor? How would he rise on the salary scale? By the way, is there a scale? Will I be in this office forever? Will I be transferred? Will I be able to do the work? Will I have a pension? Is there a retirement package? What about my children's future? Where will they go to school? Will I have enough money to pay their fees? What will be my income and is it guaranteed? Sorry, not many answers for the son of man who has nowhere to lay his head!

5. Can you follow a mysterious mission, which has no details?

By faith Abraham, when he was called to go out into a place which he should after receive for an inheritance, obeyed; and he went out, NOT KNOWING WHITHER HE WENT.

Hebrews 11:8

How would Abraham become a great nation? What kind of blessings should Abraham expect and what do they entail? Do they include a financial package? God's promises may sound vague. If you want details of what God has in store, you may not get them. When Paul was called to the ministry, the Lord told him very little. He could not know what to expect.

And he fell to the earth, and heard a voice saying unto him, Saul, Saul, why persecutest thou me?

And he said, Who art thou, Lord? And the Lord said, I am Jesus whom thou persecutest: it is hard for thee to kick against the pricks.

And he trembling and astonished said, Lord, what wilt thou have me to do? And the Lord said unto him, Arise, and go into the city, and IT SHALL BE TOLD THEE WHAT THOU MUST DO.

Acts 9:4-6

On the day of his encounter with the Lord, there were no details! The details came much later. And when the details came, they were scary! It was a mission of suffering! Wow!

And there was a certain disciple at Damascus, named Ananias; and to him said the Lord in a vision, Ananias. And he said, Behold, I am here, Lord.

And the Lord said unto him, Arise, and go into the street which is called Straight, and inquire in the house of Judas for one called Saul, of Tarsus: for, behold, he prayeth,

And hath seen in a vision a man named Ananias coming in, and putting his hand on him, that he might receive his sight.

Then Ananias answered, Lord, I have heard by many of this man, how much evil he hath done to thy saints at Jerusalem:

And here he hath authority from the chief priests to bind all that call on thy name.

But the Lord said unto him, Go thy way: for he is a chosen vessel unto me, to bear my name before the Gentiles, and kings, and the children of Israel:

FOR I WILL SHEW HIM HOW GREAT THINGS HE MUST SUFFER FOR MY NAME'S SAKE.

Acts 9:10-16

Ananias was sent to tell Paul that he was being sent on a mission of suffering. Are you ready to follow something that has no detailed plan? Are you willing to follow something in which you will suffer?

6. Can you sojourn?

By faith HE SOJOURNED in the land of promise, as in a strange country...

Hebrews 11:9

There is a Greek word "paroikeo" translated "sojourn". This word means to reside as a foreigner and to be a stranger. It is a very difficult thing to be a foreigner in a strange land. Much of God's work today involves living as a stranger amongst people in order to save them.

Do not think that the era of mission work is past. It has just begun. The reason why many think there is nothing to do is because the concept of going into a strange land has been removed by our backslidden churches.

Most pastors would not want to lose their prized members to a foreign land. No one thinks of sending people away.

We want to build one big mega church and huddle together! It is time to sojourn in a strange land for the sake of the Gospel.

7. Can you live in unsettled circumstances?

...DWELLING IN TABERNACLES with Isaac and Jacob, the heirs with him of the same promise:

Hebrews 11:9

In the secular world, people love to establish themselves, build homes and settle down. The ministry is not like that. There is not much certainty about many things. You cannot settle down. You must be ready to dwell in tabernacles (tents) all your life.

Abraham dwelt in tents because his eye was fixed on something eternal. A twenty-five year mortgage will force you to remain in a particular city. Sometimes this kind of arrangement is not compatible with the uncertainty of full-time ministry. God may require you to move on at any time.

8. Can you make your whole family follow you into this adventure?

For I know him, that he will command his children and his household after him, and they shall keep the way of the LORD...

Genesis 18:19

It is important that you bring your family along this road. Some spouses totally reject the uncertainty of it all. I have seen wives who refused to go along with their husbands. A wise man will not marry someone who shows signs of allergy to uncertainty.

The Ordination Service

Many years ago, I attended an ordination service in my city. The pastor preached powerfully and then told the story of how his wife had deserted him.

He said, "One day I came back from a ministry trip and my wife said, 'I can't take this anymore'."

She declared, "I want a normal husband and a normal home. I am tired of this kind of life."

She went on, "I want a husband who comes home at five o'clock. I want to be like every other person. I can't stay here waiting for days for my husband to come home."

She warned him, "If you don't change I'm out of this marriage and you will have to find yourself another wife."

As he ministered, he began to cry and told us how his wife eventually left him. It was very sad, and we all felt like crying. But he ended by saying he was not prepared to sacrifice his ministry for his wife's desires.

Dear friend, such is the reality of ministry. Can you make your whole household follow you on this perilous and uncertain journey?

9. Can you look for a city with foundations?

For he looked for a city which hath foundations, whose builder and maker is God.

Hebrews 11:10

Full-time ministry is all about seeking spiritual realities. We are talking about a city with foundations.

Cities like Accra, New York City, Toronto, Paris, London, Lagos, Johannesburg and Nairobi are merely cities without foundations. Sadly, most Christians are in love with these cities that have no foundations!

Christians love to write their addresses and to say they live on Martin Luther Boulevard, in Los Angeles or in Birmingham.

They don't want to be associated with despised places. They would not want anyone to know that they go to church at Kpakpo Brown Road or Ama Badua Street in Korle-Gonno.

Dear friend, neither Martin Luther Boulevard nor Kpakpo Brown Road has a foundation. It is time to lift up your eyes and see the eternal cities that have foundations. Be prepared to go anywhere because all earthly cities have no foundation anyway.

10. Can you give up your Isaac?

And he said, Take now thy son, thine only son Isaac, whom thou lovest, and get thee into the land of Moriah; and offer him there for a burnt offering upon one of the mountains which I will tell thee of.

Genesis 22:2

Isaac is the precious thing in your life. What is precious to you? Is it your job? Is it your school? Is it your beloved? Is it your lifestyle? Is it your career? Is it your American citizenship? Is it your British citizenship? Is it living in South Africa? Is it living in London?

What do you love so much? Is it your child? Is it your status in this life? Is it your security?

155

Don't Let Him Get Close

One day, some ladies were chatting. They discussed a brother who had recently left his high-earning job to come into full-time ministry. They were amazed that he could take such a decision.

They said to each other, "As for me, I would not like my husband to get near the Bishop. Everybody who becomes his friend ends up in full-time ministry! His influence is too strong."

They continued discussing, "I don't know how the wife and family will cope with this full-time thing."

Their conclusion was simple, "I really don't want my husband to go near that man."

These women were worried for their own security. The jobs their husbands had and the luxuries they provided meant everything to them. Is it too precious to sacrifice? Full-time ministry means that you leave behind the most precious things of your life.

Before you come into full-time ministry, go through these ten questions. It is an important pre-departure checklist. They will help you to be ready for life in the ministry.

Chapter 23

What it Means to Choose Full-Time Ministry

…choose you this day…

Joshua 24:15

Anyone contemplating full-time ministry is going to have to make some serious choices. Entering full-time ministry is a decision of a lifetime. You must count the cost. You must think it through. Never enter full-time ministry using lightness and frivolous reasoning.

I want you to think through six important realities that you are choosing from. Do not think that you will escape any of these realities. If Moses experienced these things, so will you.

> **By faith Moses, when he was come to years, refused to be called the son of Pharaoh's daughter;**
>
> **Choosing rather to suffer affliction with the people of God, than to enjoy the pleasures of sin for a season;**
>
> **Esteeming the reproach of Christ greater riches than the treasures in Egypt: for he had respect unto the recompence of the reward.**
>
> **By faith he forsook Egypt, not fearing the wrath of the king: for he endured, as seeing him who is invisible.**
>
> **Hebrews 11:24-27**

1. Full-time ministry is to choose something sacred.

People value different things. Some people value soccer. I hardly even know the names of famous footballers. They are not of much value to me. We who are full-time ministers value sacred things. Many people who are not into full-time ministry actually despise sacred things. The Bible teaches about Esau and describes him as a profane person.

Looking diligently lest any man fail of the grace of God; lest any root of bitterness springing up trouble you, and thereby many be defiled; Lest there be any fornicator, or profane person, as Esau, who for one morsel of meat sold his birthright.

For ye know how that afterward, when he would have inherited the blessing, he was rejected: for he found no place of repentance, though he sought it carefully with tears.

Hebrews 12:15-17

The word "profane" is the Greek word "bebelos". It is a word used to describe Esau as an irreligious man and a despiser of sacred things. Esau despised sacred things because he was not a spiritual man. Spiritual people called to the ministry place a value on holy things.

The account in the Scripture above shows us that Esau had the opportunity to receive an inheritance, a blessing and a birthright. By simply accepting the gift and position he would have had an inheritance, a blessing and a birthright. This is what full-time ministry is about. It is all about handling sacred things.

Unfortunately, many people do not value sacred things. They actually despise them and look down on them. I believe in these sacred spiritual things. A word spoken over my life means everything to me. The unearned and undeserved position God has given me means everything to me. I cherish the presence of these unquantifiable sacred blessings.

Years ago, I took some brethren on a trip to attend a Benny Hinn meeting. It was an exciting time and we all looked forward to it. When we got to the meeting, I was ushered on stage whilst my friends were given very good seats in the first few rows. The auditorium was packed and thousands of people were turned away. We were truly privileged to have our special seats.

There was excitement in the air and the congregation buzzed with expectation. Suddenly the worship began and Benny Hinn walked onto the stage. I was so excited to be right there at the ringside. In a few minutes, Benny Hinn was ministering.

As the service progressed, I could not help thinking about how fortunate I was to be on stage and how blessed my other friends were to be about five rows from the very front. I looked across into the congregation to see if they were enjoying everything as much as I was. To my surprise, one of them was fast asleep with his head bent over and his mouth hanging open.

I thought I was not seeing aright! How could somebody sleep in such an atmosphere? Was it not a special occasion to be sitting live in a Benny Hinn miracle service? The service was not more than ten minutes old. How tired could anyone be at this time? I felt I was so blessed and it was a sacred moment for me. But somehow, it was such a boring moment to my friend that he had fallen asleep.

The point I am making is that people value different things. Perhaps if a politician or some non-Christian motivational speaker were on stage, he would have been wide awake. But the healing and miracle service of Benny Hinn was simply not interesting enough to him.

2. Full time ministry is a choice to reject greatness in the secular world.

By faith Moses...refused to be called the son of Pharaoh's daughter,

Hebrews 11:24

Incredibly, Moses refused to be called the king's son. It was a rejection of earthly honour and prestige. Are you ready for that? Are you ready to forsake every human title and acknowledgement?

When I chose to be in full-time ministry, it was a rejection of human greatness. I would never be called a cardio-thoracic surgeon. I would never be called a neurologist or a psychiatrist. The medical and academic fraternity would never honour me. Professors would now exclude me from their circles. I would be associated with priests, pastors and other religious weirdos. This was the choice I made when I chose full-time ministry.

3. Full-time ministry is a choice for affliction.

...Moses...Choosing rather to suffer affliction with the people of God, than to enjoy the pleasures of sin for a season;

Hebrews 11:25

There are certain sufferings that go along with full-time ministry. To choose full-time ministry is to choose affliction. I constantly tell people who are coming into full-time ministry to expect poverty.

There is no biblical basis for a life of luxury. All the Bible has to say are things to do with crosses, sacrifices, sufferings and afflictions.

We cannot say anything against the truth but for the truth. The affliction of full-time ministry for you may be different from the affliction that I experienced. Whatever the case, you will suffer some affliction. You must accept that you will never enjoy certain pleasures in this life. Are you ready for that?

I Will Never Forget

I always remember when I took the decision for full-time ministry. I knew I would never live in a home like the one I had known in my childhood; a large house in a prime area with many rooms, a big garden, a swimming pool, a summer hut and lots of space. I estimated that the highest kind of comfort I would ever have would be a tiny two-bedroom flat in a poor suburb of Accra, Ghana.

I also thought that I would never travel on an airplane again. I knew that my days of flying were over. I would never have enough money to buy a ticket for the rest of my life. I genuinely took that decision when I came into full-time ministry. Poverty and affliction is a definite choice that you make when you choose full-time ministry.

4. Full time ministry is to esteem, and treasure reproach.

Esteeming the reproach...

Hebrews 11:26

From the time I chose to be in full-time ministry, it became important for me to value reproach.

One day, I heard that someone had called me "Satan". Instead of getting angry, I knelt down and thanked God for the honour of being insulted with the same insults that my Saviour had received. Jesus was associated with Beelzebub by unbelieving critics.

But when the Pharisees heard it, they said, This fellow doth not cast out devils, but by Beelzebub the prince of the devils.

Matthew 12:24

You must value every insult and criticism. One professor asked his students whether I was mad for starting a church whilst in medical school. But I was grateful that somebody was enquiring whether I was mad because Paul had also been accused of madness. I am glad to be associated with the reproaches of people like Christ Jesus and Paul.

Festus, a ruler before whom Paul was arraigned asked Paul whether he was mad.

While Paul was saying this in his defense, Festus said in a loud voice, "Paul, you are out of your mind! Your great learning is driving you mad." But Paul said, "I am not out of my mind, most excellent Festus, but I utter words of sober truth."

Acts 26:24-25, NASB

Somebody said, "I can't stand insults. I do not like it when people talk about me."

Then I said, "Then you cannot be in the ministry."

Ministry work involves people having a field day discussing, analyzing and criticizing you!

5. Full time ministry is to choose to respect the rewards of Heaven.

...for he had respect unto the recompense of the reward.

Hebrews 11:26

To come into full-time ministry, you must have a great regard for heavenly rewards. You must respect the concept of receiving white gowns, crowns and white stones. If all you respect are earthly appointment letters with fat remuneration packages from the bank, you are not fit for full-time ministry and are unlikely to succeed in it.

There are no such appointment letters for full-time ministry. There is no promise of cars, houses or fat bonuses. Moses respected the thought of rewards in Heaven. "For he had respect unto the recompense of the reward" (Hebrews 11:26).

6. Full time ministry is to choose to forsake the world system.

By faith he forsook Egypt...

Hebrews 11:27

Coming into full-time ministry also involves forsaking the world. In the world salaries are guaranteed every month. Moses forsook the life in the Egyptian palace and opted for the wilderness. Can you imagine what it felt like as he walked away from the glorious city of Ramses into the dark frightening desert? That is what full-time ministry is all about.

It is to walk away from a glamorous job in a glassy bank building to a simple church building where even the mice are said to be poor.

7. Full time ministry is to choose not to fear the king.

...Not fearing the wrath of the king...

Hebrews 11:27

Who is the king in your life? Is it your father? Or is it your mother? Is the king the uncle who paid your school fees? Or is it your very own wife? How will these people punish me for my decision to be in full-time ministry? Will they stop their financial support? Will they strike my name out of their family? To be in full-time ministry, you must overcome the fear of every kind of king!

Full-time ministry involves conquering your raging fears. It is truly a frightening thing to abandon everything and enter into full-time ministry.

Questions abound: Will I survive? Will I have food to eat? Will I ever drive a car? Will I ever be happy? Will my children ever go to school? By how much will my life change? What will people think of me? These are just a few of the fears you may have but the Lord will deliver you from all your fears (Psalm 34:4).

8. Full time ministry is to choose to follow invisible things.

...for he endured, as seeing him who is invisible.

Hebrews 11:27

Moses endured full-time ministry. He did this by looking at invisible things. Once again, it is only by focusing on unseen eternal realities that full-time ministry is possible. Today's church can hardly produce missionaries.

It is a materialistic church whose trust is in this world's physical wealth. Both pastors and congregation are earthly-minded with dreams of material success and wealth. How can such people look at invisible things? How can such people send young men to jungles, villages to win the forgotten souls of this world?

What are invisible things? They are Heaven, Hell, angels, devils, eternity, eternal rewards and all the things spoken of in the book of Revelation. God Himself is invisible. Jesus is also invisible.

What are the visible things? They are cities, buildings, banks, money, wealth, clothes, diamonds, gold, cars and the like. You cannot do full-time ministry with your eyes on visible things.

Lift up your eyes and see the invisible, then you will be well able to last in full-time ministry!

Chapter 24

The Privileges of
Full-Time Ministers

Full-time ministry affords the minister some of the highest privileges ever given to human beings. There is nothing more precious than these blessings.

1. **Full-time ministers have the privilege of no longer following after dung.**

   ...and do count them but dung, that I may win Christ,

   Philippians 3:8

   The call to full-time ministry delivers you from the pursuit of dung. Coprophilia is a disease in which a person loves watching people defecate or loves to be defecated upon. This is a terrible disease - to love faeces.

   If someone delivered you from coprophilia would you not be grateful? According to Paul the pursuit of Christ with the attendant loss of all things (full-time ministry) is like being delivered from following faeces.

2. **Full-time ministers have gained the privilege of being found in Him.**

   And be found in him...

   Philippians 3:9

   Instead of being found in the library, the market or the bank you can be found in the presence of the Lord. What a privilege this is - to be found in Him!

3. **Full-time ministers have gained the privilege of knowing Him.**

   That I may know him...

   Philippians 3:10

By coming to work for God and with God, the great blessing will be that you should know Him better. If you work with someone, you get to know the person.

Whilst others are getting to know the Managing Director better, you are getting to know the Lord better. Whilst others are getting closer to Professors you are getting closer to God and to His servants.

4. Full-time ministers have the privilege of becoming fellow sufferers with Christ.

...and the fellowship of his sufferings...

Philippians 3:10

What a privilege it is to share in the sufferings of someone great. It will earn you a crown when it really matters. Anyone who suffers with an honourable man will never be forgotten.

Abiathar Suffers with David

King David appointed Solomon to be heir of his throne. Unfortunately, some people (including Abiathar) tried to displace Solomon and ascend the throne. The evil plot was quelled and Solomon became king and took his rightful place.

Solomon executed all the people who tried to usurp his throne, except one person - Abiathar the priest.

Solomon told Abiathar that he deserved to die. However, instead of executing him, he spared his life for one reason - Abiathar had been through much suffering with his father David.

Then to Abiathar the priest the king said, "Go to Anathoth to your own field, for you deserve to die; but I will not put you to death at this time, because you carried the ark of the Lord GOD before my father David, and because you were afflicted in everything with which my father was afflicted."

So Solomon dismissed Abiathar from being priest to the LORD, in order to fulfill the word of the LORD,

which He had spoken concerning the house of Eli in Shiloh.

1 Kings 2:26-27, NASB

The Disciples Suffer with Christ

Jesus said the same thing to His disciples. They had been through much suffering with Him and he would never forget it. He promised them special rewards just because they had suffered with him.

Ye are they which have continued with me in my temptations. And I appoint unto you a kingdom, as my Father hath appointed unto me;

Luke 22:28-29

One of the privileges of full-time ministry is to join Christ in the shame and humiliation of true ministry. Surely, sharing the shame and suffering of Christ will not be in vain.

5. **Full-time ministers are privileged to fight for a glorious resurrection.**

If by any means I might attain unto the resurrection of the dead.

Philippians 3:11

Instead of being presumptuous, full-time ministers fight to ensure they are part of the glorious resurrection.

6. **Full-time ministers are delivered from complacency.**

Not as though I had already attained, either were already perfect: but I follow after...

Philippians 3:12

The lack of labourers and harvesters becomes apparent when you become a full-time minister.

Through full-time ministry, your personal inadequacies are revealed. The daunting task of ministry removes the feeling of being perfect.

The harvest fields of lost souls weigh on the true minister. You will not be able to say you have arrived. You will never feel accomplished no matter how much you work. This reality saves you from the sin of complacency.

What a privilege to be delivered from the deception of thinking we are something that we are not!

7. Full-time ministers have the privilege of attaining the reason for which they were saved.

...that I may apprehend that for which also I am apprehended of Christ Jesus.

Philippians 3:12

When I was a student, the aging founder of the Church of Pentecost preached to the university fellowship of his denomination from this text. That is how I always remember this Scripture. I always imagine this seasoned warrior saying, "That I may apprehend that for which I was apprehended!"

Sadly, most Christians never apprehend that for which they were apprehended. Is this not the most important thing in the world? To accomplish the things for which Christ saved you?

Why did He save you? Why did He love you? Why did He call you? Why you and not somebody else?

Thank God for a divine opportunity to attain to your divine destiny!

8. Full-time ministers have a chance to forget the past.

...forgetting those things which are behind...

Philippians 3:13

Full-time ministry will swallow up your life. There will be no time or energy to remember the past. Paul's past was wiped away as he pursued the Lord in full-time ministry. He was now able to press towards the things of God that lay ahead.

9. Full-time ministers can have a special prize.

I press toward the mark for the prize of the high calling of God in Christ Jesus.

Philippians 3:13-14

All full-time ministers are privileged to target the prize of the high calling. This is not the prize for the best student in French. It is the prize of the high calling. It must be something special and I am blessed to aim for this wonderful prize.

Chapter 25

Why Some People Leave the Work of Ministry

But we are not of them who draw back...

Hebrews 10:39

Years ago, I sat in a restaurant with a seasoned minister of God. He had built a large church in a city and had several other branch churches. As we chatted, he told me something that stunned me.

He said, "I have decided to leave the ministry and go into business."

He explained, "I find the ministry boring. It does not challenge me anymore."

Then he said, "I can't imagine myself doing this for the rest of my life."

He told me how he had decided to go to university so that he could accomplish many more things.

I was bewildered, as I had never met anyone like that.

To me, coming into ministry was the greatest step of my life. Leaving medicine behind was such a big upward step.

I wondered, "Why would anyone do something like that?" What would make someone who is successful in ministry abandon everything and return to the secular world?

Well, I was to find out that he was not the first, and neither would he be the last to return.

Types of Returnees

Type 1: The Subtle Type

Some people partially desert the ministry because of attractions to other vocations.

I have heard of different ministers going into politics, business, medical work, social work, government work and all sorts of other occupations.

There are several subtle defections from ministry. Actually, many people depart from ministry in their hearts before they get involved in business, social work and politics.

In a sense, the ministry becomes a thing of the past. It no longer consumes their whole being as it used to.

Sadly, the work of the ministry is relegated to the position of a stepchild. They maintain the title Reverend and continue to pastor their churches, but they have actually metamorphosed into part-time ministers and part-time something else. Surely, there has been a subtle but significant shift from true ministry.

Is There Nothing to Do?

All these subtle defections from the ministry are done against the background of six billion souls waiting to be won to Jesus. As nations fall to Islam, Christian ministers charged with spreading the Gospel rather find time for a host of other things!

Ironically, as millions continue to die and go to Hell, the urgency of our calling seems to be weaker. Perhaps backslidden pastors who are possessed with the spirit of worldliness and who value wealth more than the anointing lead the church.

It is because we are a backslidden church that the idea of substituting the ministry of the cross and the blood of Jesus with business, politics or humanitarian works can even be suggested in the church community.

Type 2: The Demas Type

For Demas has forsaken me, having loved this present world...

2 Timothy 4:10, NKJV

Demas was in full-time ministry with the Apostle Paul. Yet he forsook Paul and returned to his old life. Paul explained why this had happened: Demas had loved this present world. No one who loves this present world will do well in full-time ministry. You must not love this earthly, physical world. Your heart must be fixed on eternal things.

The worst type of person to mistakenly be in full-time ministry is someone who loves this present world. If you love the glamour and wealth of the cities of this world, how can you be sent to villages where the poor and needy await salvation?

Sadly, many Christians are in love with this world and they are incompatible with full-time ministry. A lover of cars, money, clothes, and houses should not apply to work in full-time ministry. The ministry is not a place for people with earthly goals. Your earthly ambitions will soon be in conflict with the goals of ministry.

Do you desire fame and acknowledgement from the world? Do you desire earthly laurels? Do you want to be seen as one of the young, upwardly progressive people of this era? Well, that is not compatible with full-time ministry. Full-time ministry will lead to rejection by the world.

The medical community from which I emanate did not hail or praise me for entering into full-time ministry. They despised me and called me names. One doctor asked if I had gone mad. I don't blame them. I am not trying to impress them.

Type 3: The Lot's Wife Type

Remember Lot's wife.

Luke 17:32

But his wife looked back behind him, and she became a pillar of salt.

Genesis 19:26, NKJV

Lot's wife turned into a pillar of salt because she looked into the past. Do not look back; otherwise, your ministry will freeze. You cannot have the same friends, the same cars, the same income, the same clothes, the same pastimes that you had when you were in the world. If you look back longingly at these things, you have troubled yourself.

He Looked Back

One day, a brother who was in full-time ministry began complaining about his work. In one of his outbursts, he made a pronouncement, which was revealing.

He blurted out, "If I was still working at King Kong Fishing Company, I would be earning thousands of dollars by now."

You see, this fellow used to be a Manager for King Kong and it was now five years since he had resigned and entered into full-time ministry. He was looking back at his income. He was considering what his income might have been. When you look back, you have all sorts of imaginations about what you could have become. This paralyses you in full-time ministry and makes you want to return.

If we all look back and imagine what we might have been, our ministries may come to a grinding halt. Looking back is not an option once you are in full-time ministry.

Type 4: The Mark Type

Barnabas wanted to take John, called Mark, along with them also.

But Paul kept insisting that they should not take him along who had deserted them in Pamphylia and had not gone with them to the work.

Acts 15:37-38, NASB

173

Mark is an example of someone who abandoned the ministry midstream. I have seen this several times. These people suddenly resign from full-time ministry without much explanation. They abruptly disengage from the ministry without obvious reason. This type of desertion is distressing as it is never clear why the individual is departing.

Once, I had a pastor I loved dearly and to whom I had assigned a very important job. Everything seemed to be going well until I suddenly got a letter by which he resigned from the ministry. I found out later that this fellow was offended about various things.

Several other ministers who have behaved in this "Mark" fashion had hidden reasons in their hearts.

And then shall many be offended, and shall betray one another, and shall hate one another.

Matthew 24:10

Alas, unhealed wounds are not compatible with the priesthood. No minister will flourish if he keeps bitterness within.

I tell you, unforgiveness will remove you from the ministry faster than you can imagine. Unforgiveness and a lack of communication are the cause of this kind of desertion.

Type 5: The Peter Type

Simon Peter said to them, "I am going fishing." They said to him, "We are going with you also." They went out and immediately got into the boat, and that night they caught nothing.

John 21:3, NKJV

After Peter had received training for three years, he decided to go back to fishing. Peter's return to fishing was one of his most unfortunate choices. He carried along with him people that looked up to him.

This is the type of desertion in which people do not appreciate their ministerial training. Such people do not realize the investments that have been made in their lives. They disregard years of Bible school training and simply put it aside.

The Bible School Picture

Years ago, Dr Yonggi Cho told a story of how he found an old picture of his Bible school mates. He noted that most of them were dead. Just a couple of them were still alive and those were the ones still in ministry. You see, instead of preaching, many of them had become welders, carpenters, drivers, etc. Bible school training had not meant much to some of them.

In the "Peter type" of desertion, the person does not know the greatness of his calling! The entire church of Jesus Christ depended on Peter becoming a rock and a foundation. Yet here he was fishing. And he was not alone, but he was fishing with all the other rocks and foundations of the church. Mercy!

How was the church to be built if Peter returned to fishing? Did the three years with Christ mean nothing? Did all the teachings and private discussions found in the book of John mean nothing? What was Peter looking for?

You Will Not Prosper When You Return

Peter caught nothing that night. He was looking for fish but there was no fish to be found for the returning apostle.

Jesus called out and told the struggling defectors what to do. Once again, our Lord proved that we can do nothing without him, including our professions. They ran to the shore and found Jesus grilling the very fish they were looking for.

God knows what we need. There is no need for us to abandon our calling to chase our needs.

It is only when they fished on the instructions of Jesus that it yielded anything. Everything else was useless.

Simon Peter said to them, "I am going fishing." They said to him, "We will also come with you." They went

out and got into the boat; and that night they caught nothing.

But when the day was now breaking, Jesus stood on the beach; yet the disciples did not know that it was Jesus.

So Jesus said to them, "Children, you do not have any fish, do you?" They answered Him, "No."

And He said to them, "Cast the net on the right-hand side of the boat and you will find a catch." So they cast, and then they were not able to haul it in because of the great number of fish.

Therefore that disciple whom Jesus loved said to Peter, "It is the Lord." So when Simon Peter heard that it was the Lord, he put his outer garment on (for he was stripped for work), and threw himself into the sea.

But the other disciples came in the little boat, for they were not far from the land, but about one hundred yards away, dragging the net full of fish.

So when they got out on the land, they saw a charcoal fire already laid and fish placed on it, and bread.

Jesus said to them, "Bring some of the fish which you have now caught."

Simon Peter went up and drew the net to land, full of large fish, a hundred and fifty-three; and although there were so many, the net was not torn.

Jesus said to them, "Come and have breakfast." None of the disciples ventured to question Him, "Who are You?" knowing that it was the Lord.

Jesus came and took the bread and gave it to them, and the fish likewise.

John 21:3-13, NASB

Sheep or Fish?

It was after this that Jesus asked, "Do you love me?" When Peter said, "I love you", Jesus asked him to go back to ministry work. In other words, "Please don't go back to fishing. Concentrate on the sheep and feed them." How many ministers have left the sheep and gone back to fishing? Perhaps countless have. Could it be that we do not love Jesus anymore? May God have mercy on our souls!

Type 6: The Bored Type

Then shall we know, if we follow on to know the LORD...

Hosea 6:3

There is a type of desertion in ministry, which comes from not continuing to follow the Lord. It is easy to start out in the ministry but it is not that easy to continue. To be steadfast in ministry is important.

Steadfastness is a word borrowed from the navy. It speaks of the ability to stay on course. It also speaks of the ability to come back to course after you have drifted off. Many ministers do not have steadfastness. They cannot fulfil the calling of a pastor. It takes steadfastness to continue preaching divine and mystical truths in spite of the pressure to change the message and make it more "relevant".

Following the Lord is an exciting adventure. It is a quest without parallel. You will find yourself running, fighting, thinking, surviving and strategizing all the time.

Paul described the tension of ministry in the second book of Corinthians. He said,

For we do not want you to be unaware, brethren, of our affliction which came to us in Asia, that we were burdened excessively, beyond our strength, so that we despaired even of life; indeed, we had the sentence of death within ourselves so that we would not trust in ourselves, but in God who raises the dead; who delivered us from so great a peril of death, and will deliver us, He on whom we have set our hope. And He will yet deliver us,

2 Corinthians 1:8-10, NASB

How can ministry be boring? It is because you have ceased to follow the Lord that ministry has become boring to you. Many have taken detours because their eyes are set on natural goals rather than God-given tasks.

I feel no rest and I feel no ease after all these years in ministry. There is always a certain kind of tension within me. It is as though I just began. The closer I get to God the more worried I am for my state.

The whole world lies in wickedness! Billions of souls are waiting for us!

The forgotten ones sleep and awake everyday in their villages hoping it will be the day when the good news will be brought to them.

Seeking for the Lord in full-time ministry will never be boring. It will challenge you to the very core.

Do not let any minister deceive you into thinking that there is time and space for earthly pursuits. It is time to spend and be spent!

Paul's last words do not give the impression of someone who was bored. His last words do not give the impression of someone looking for a new job.

He had no time for a political or social role in Rome where he was a citizen. You can sense the exhaustion, the intensity and the dedication to the original purpose.

For I am now ready to be offered, and the time of my departure is at hand.

I have fought a good fight, I have finished my course, I have kept the faith:

2 Timothy 4:6-7

Full-time ministry is the best thing that could ever happen to you. There is no parallel to this high calling. There is no greater opportunity that a person could have.

I highly recommend that your life be spent in absolute surrender and full-time commitment to the purpose and prize of the Gospel!

Dear friend, to the making of many books there is no end. Please be satisfied with these few words.